THE
BOOTLEGGER'S
LADY

THE BOOTLEGGER'S LADY

Ed Sager & Mike Frye

hancock

house

ISBN 0-88839-976-6
Copyright © 1984 Edward Sager and Mike Frye

Third Printing 1993

Cataloging in Publication Data
Sager, Edward and Frye, Mike
   The bootlegger's lady

   Bibliography: p.
   ISBN 0-88839-976-6

1. Frye, Edith. 2. Pioneers–British Columbia–Biogra-
   phy. I. Frye, Mike. II. Title
FC3825.1.F7S241984 971.1'03'0924 C83-091327-0
F1088.S241984

Production: Dorothy Forbes
Production assistant: Jane Gueho
Cover art: Glen Russell

Published simultaneously in Canada and the United States by

HANCOCK HOUSE PUBLISHERS LTD.
19313 Zero Avenue, Surrey, B.C. V4P 1M7
(604) 538-1114 Fax (604) 538-2262

HANCOCK HOUSE PUBLISHERS
1431 Harrison Avenue, Box 959, Blaine, WA 98231-0959
(206) 354-6953 Fax (604) 538-2262

Table of Contents

Acknowledgments

Mary Bawlf, curator, Kamloops Museum
Grace Carlisle, cousin of Edith Frye
D.W.H. Creighton, grandson of Mr. Justice Murphy
Ella Frye
Sadie Frye (Mrs. Mike Frye)
David F. Hurd, Planetarium Scientist, H.R. MacMillan
   Planetarium
T.W. Knight, District Registrar, Kamloops
Frances Frye Knudson
Jim McCauley, Bella Coola
David B. Mason, Assistant Provincial Archivist
M. Patricia Murphy, granddaughter of Mr. Justice Murphy
Howard "Slim" O'Hagan
Charles E. Rice, Registrar of Deeds, Rolette County,
   North Dakota, cousin of Edith Frye
Frank E. Vyzralek, North Dakota State Archivist
David Williams, QC

For those whom God to ruin has design'd,
He fits for fate, and first destroys their mind.

(John Dryden, 1631-1700)

Oh, what was your name in the States?
Was it Thompson or Johnson or Bates?
Did you murder your wife
and fly for your life?
Say, what was your name in the States?

(favorite ditty of the Forty-niners)

Foreword

The pioneers were not angels. The first to press into the wilderness of western Canada were for the most part unruly men, adapted to a harsh land and ferocious conditions. They lived outside the law by accident of geography, and some because they would not be bound by the conventions of civilized men. In the vanguard were the bootleggers; whisky led the way.

The legend of the frontier outlaw is rooted in fact. As late as 1904, Butch Cassidy and the Sundance Kid could be seen bicycling in the streets of Fort Worth, Texas. The figure of the lone bad man, though, is mostly fiction. Fertility is a requirement for long-term survival on any frontier. Even outlaws married, cleared homesteads, planted crops and raised families.

Frederick Charles Frye was, according to one daughter, "an outlaw; one of the real old-time bad men." He was no mere criminal. Several inches short of five feet tall, he was a man of extraordinary physical strength in an age when most men worked hard. His character was ruled by his own passions; he recognized few laws outside of his own. He was both a bootlegger and a respected businessman known for his remarkable energy; well-liked when sober and feared when he had liquor; a father and philanderer; gunfighter and enthusiastic amateur actor; a dangerous brawler and a resourceful guide. The ungoverned passions which made him a terrible man also lent him the strength to tear a homestead out of the wilderness and prosper where others failed. For all his flaws, Fred Frye was a successful pioneer, and his descendants owe him that legacy if little else.

To surmount both the wild country and such a wild man, his wife had to be stronger than both. Such strength tempered by gentleness is an extraordinary combination. Edith Julia Frye possessed both qualities in abundance. She followed her husband half way across the continent driving a heavy freight wagon, pregnant every other year; bore him nine children and raised them nearly single-handed; endured his philandering, bootlegging, drinking and unpredictable rages; and survived him.

It is more than half a century since this story took place. In such a span of time many things may be forgotten or put out of mind. Nevertheless, a sound skeleton of events still exists, in archives, museums, citizenship files and land registries stretching from North Dakota to British Columbia. Most importantly, Mike Frye, probably the first white child born west of the Yellowhead Pass, recorded much of his parents' travails.

Some of this account is, necessarily, speculation. No record tells who it was that Fred Frye shot during a drunken quarrel in North Dakota; the crime probably never came to the attention of the authorities. Only his wife's testimony and the recollections of a cousin who was a small girl at the time throw any light on that dark deed. Mystery still shrouds the death of a railroad man on the Frye homestead, although one of the children was a witness to the bloody brawl in which the man died. Rumors about the slaying still circulate in the North Thompson River valley.

The description of the blind pig in McCumber, North Dakota, is based on historical accounts and personal recollections, but whether Fred Frye maintained an illegal speakeasy in his livery stable cannot be ascertained. Certainly, he made and sold moonshine in North Dakota, as did many others at the time, but we do not know exactly where or how he operated.

The country the Fryes traversed in their six-year emigration from North Dakota to British Columbia is well-described in journals of the time, and of course, the major geological features are still there for anyone to see. Even the ford they crossed at Tete Jaune Cache can still be located, within a few hundred yards of the present Highway 5 bridge over the Fraser River.

This story may reopen old wounds long thought to have healed. Some of the Frye children were reluctant to tell of the abuse they suffered at the hands of a drink-crazed father; in the twisted temper of our time, the victims of some crimes carry a greater shame than the perpetrator.

They feared that their children and grandchildren might suffer the same ostracism they experienced. Many other pioneer women, they maintain, did as much as their mother. What seems incredible now was commonplace then; people simply coped as best they could.

It was not my intention to cause anyone pain, particularly those who freely shared an experience they had held secret for over half a century. I cannot agree that their story should not be told, however. Little has been written about the tough, enduring men, and virtually nothing about the indomitable women who opened the raw new land called British Columbia and populated it. Few pioneers left any written testament, not because what they did was not extraordinary, but because they were too busy simply trying to survive. Yet their accomplishments are no less significant than those of the reputed nation-builders about whom volumes have been written.

The children of Fred and Edith Frye belong to this story, but it is not only theirs. We are all the sons or daughters of pioneers, and history belongs to all of us. If this story is not told it will be lost, and that would be the greater pity.

Ed Sager

Blind Pigs & Bootlegging

Moonlight shone upon the North Dakota plain, by the year 1906 already defined by a geometry of roads and cultivated fields. Clots of cattle, black in the cold light, clustered around the fenced-in hayricks beside the farmhouses and barns that dotted the Rolette County prairie. The cattle, turned out to forage on the stubble emerging from the patchy snow, stood heads low, tails to the steady, damp wind, unable to reach the few remaining straws of the ricks.

Moonshine more potent than the silvery light from above flowed across the plain. Stills sprouted like mushrooms in any dark, hidden place: beneath stables, in old barns, hidden in woody copses and inaccessible brakes. Bootlegging was big business in North Dakota, which had entered the Union in 1889 with a prohibition clause in its constitution. The state remained legally dry until the failure of national prohibition in 1933. Rolette County, with an international border close at hand, was a moonshiner's paradise during both the Canadian and the American prohibition periods.

Early in 1906 a new livery stable towered over the

street in the small new railroad town of McCumber, Rolette County. Yellow lamplight spilled through the wide cracks between the plank walls into the muddy street where half a dozen wagons and teams and several saddlehorses stamped and snorted in the chilly air. Rents in the temporary canvas roof breathed smoke and steam lit from below, like geisers from Hell.

Inside, a large brass potbelly stove belched heat into the rude room, flames scorching the isinglass peephole in the firedoor. The stovepipe, supported by slings of wire, ran the length of the room to a vent, leaking smoke and fine ash from the joints as the stove snorted and grumbled. Hanging lanterns did little to dispel the haze, thickened by the pipes and cigars of the dozen or so men who stood by the plank and sawhorse bar.

The back room of the livery stable was a *blind pig,* a speakeasy. The name was derived from *hog ranch,* frontier slang for a brothel. In wet states, legitimate saloons offered a drink, the latest jokes, a place where a traveler could check his bags, play cards, even have a bath. Blind pigs had a more singular purpose: stand-up, falling-down drinking. A drinking man's code evolved from stern necessity: never drink alone, and never abandon a friend who has passed out.

The bootlegger stood behind the bar. Fred Frye, who stood several inches shy of five feet tall, was known to be a strong man in an age when brutal outdoor work was the fate of most men. His round-jawed face under a thick handlebar mustache was angled by lumps of muscle. His coat, cut down from a taller man's to accommodate his wide shoulders, hung nearly to his knees. He had large, even teeth, unusual in days of minimal dental care.

The crowd of farmers, most of them men with time on their hands until the fields dried enough for spring sowing, listened closely to his words.

"So an acting troupe comes to town," Frye was saying, "and only half an hour before the show, the lead actress gets sick and can't go on. The manager runs out into the street and stops the first nice-looking woman he finds.

14

" 'Ten dollars if you'll stand in for my leading lady,' he tells her. 'All you have to do is step out onto the stage, you're shot by the villain, then throw up your arms and fall down dead.'

"She says she'll do it, and when the curtain goes up she does her part to perfection. The villain drops his piece and says, 'Oh my God, what have I done?'

"And somebody in the back yells out, 'You damn fool, you've gone and killed the only whore in town!' "

There was general laughter. Fred Frye was known to be a sporting man, and was well-liked, at least when not in the grip of liquor. His short stature did not cause much comment as most men were closer to five feet tall than six in those days. But even in rough company, men made room for Fred Frye.

The laughter stopped abruptly as a fight broke out at one of the tables. Frye slipped under the bar and headed toward the action as one of the two antagonists clubbed the other to the floor. Frye's fist caught the standing man behind the ear and he rebounded off the wall, still conscious and fighting mad. He swung at the short man.

Frye ducked under the blow as his nose cleared and odors poured in: sour sweat, horses, tobacco, whisky, smoke. Something primitive swept over him. The muscles of his thick neck and shoulders rose like tautened cables and he sunk a fist below the farmer's belt. The taller man doubled over, coughing a spray of whisky and spittle into Frye's face. Frye picked him up by crotch and throat and threw him down the room. He landed face first and slid into the big stove. The stovepipes collapsed, filling the room with soot. Smoke bellowed from the stove.

"Fire!" someone bellowed.

Frye slipped through the choking smoke and kicked the fallen man in the head, then slung him out into the muddy street. Someone ran in with a bucket of water and flung it into the stove. A gush of steam went up and the blind pig emptied. Men scrambled for their horses.

"It ain't the size of the man in the fight," joked one onlooker, "it's the size of the fight in the man."

Fred Frye was an atavism, a throwback who possessed a physical strength unique to only a few in-

15

dividuals in any generation. He could easily heave a four-hundred-pound flour barrel onto a freight wagon unassisted. But there was something else about him that made him a fearful opponent in a brawl.

In all of mankind there lies at the core of oneself a primitive force millions of years old: the rhinencephalon or "smelling brain." This legacy from primitive man controls primal behavior such as anger, fear, attack and lust. When in the grip of that ancient force a ninety-pound woman can lift a car off her injured child.

Man's modern brain, the cerebrum, which overlies the rhinencephalon, is only a hundred thousand years old. In Fred Frye, that ancient force was close to the surface. Decades later he might have been analyzed as a psychomotor epileptic, an individual subject to violent seizures when his primitive brain was triggered. Among the agents which could precipitate such an attack were fusel oils, the mixture of poisonous aldehydes and ketones found in moonshine whisky.

He had been born in California in 1872. His father had fled pogroms in Odessa on the Black Sea around the time the War Between the States had ground to a bloody halt.

Like so many refugees before him, he found his way to the new land, arriving in New York. But the cold winters did not suit him, a warm-blooded man used to the Mediterranean-like shores of the Black Sea, and he worked his way to the more moderate climate of the west coast. There he met and married a young Spanish woman whose family, the Condocovioues, owned a number of theatres and gambling establishments in the San Francisco area. The couple moved to Seattle, bought land and prospered.

They had several children, and young Fred was a problem even in his teens, uncontrollable and violent. Before he had reached maturity he was too much for his parents to handle, and he was cast out. He graduated to the logging camps where he became an expert in infighting, from eye gouging to ear biting, while keeping his own organs intact.

Smart and quick to make decisions, he soon saw that

the back-breaking labor in the tall timber could leave even the strongest man crippled. The peasant art of distilling was in his blood and he easily gravitated to the ancient trade. There was always a ready market for liquor in the mining and logging camps. Booze blunted the edge of a harsh existence; whisky made life endurable for men who worked twelve to eighteen hours a day, subsisting on fried beef and biscuits.

Young Fred Frye developed an uncanny sense for when it was time to move on. He migrated east, usually one jump ahead of the law, until he came to North Dakota. There contraband liquor sales was a very viable business. Grain could easily be bought from crooked elevator operators who habitually short-changed their farm customers. There was ready access to the thirsty market of Montana by means of the railroad. Butte's notorious Galena Street was a line of tents, shacks, gambling dens and whorehouses. The established brothels published "blue books" offering "boarders" all the comforts of "home" and listed their "entertainers" by name and race.

The moonshine traveled by thousands of ingenious streams to the customers. In one instance the bootleggers unwittingly repeated a page of history. A thousand years earlier, Christians who discovered the relics of St. Mark in Alexandria smuggled the holy remains to Venice concealed in a load of pork, an abomination to the infidel customs guards. The bootleggers stuffed their unholy spirits inside hog and beef carcasses to deliver them to the thirsty faithful.

Outwardly respectable, Fred Frye invested in legitimate business and was active in amateur theatre groups in northern North Dakota. Just before the turn of the century he met Edith Julia Bronson, whose family owned substantial farm properties in Rolette County. Four years older and a bit taller than him, dark-skinned with very bright, dark brown eyes, Edith Bronson at twenty-seven was facing a barren future of spinsterhood.

Her forebears had come to the new world shortly after Charles I was beheaded. Her ancestors had fought in the American Revolution, and her maternal grandfather, Simon S. Rice, had fought in the Civil War.

The family came to North Dakota when the railroads opened up the country, and established farms in southern Rolette County near the Pierce County line. Edith's mother, Helen, had been married before, to one Tom Berry, who mysteriously left, never to return. Thereafter she married Julius Abraham Bronson, called Joel, and had four daughters by him. After her death Julius left the children with their grandparents, Simon and Abigail Harrington Rice.

He returned with another daughter, named Julia, by an unrecorded liaison. The grandparents played a large part in bringing up the five little girls.

By the time she met Fred Frye, Edith was the last of the daughters at home. Two of her sisters, Suzan and Elizabeth, had married brothers by the name of Hardenburg and gone to Montana to live.

Edith and Fred were married in 1900 in Rolla, the county seat, on the Great Northern's line from Devil's Lake. Edith's Aunt and Uncle Rice held a supper for them with music and dancing, as her uncle played the violin.

A year after the wedding Edith presented Fred with a daughter, Myrtle. They traveled to Willow City to have their portrait taken. The pose was one often used when the man was shorter than the woman: Edith stood while Fred sat, with the baby on his knee. Edith looked tired and was a bit out of focus; Fred was smooth-skinned and mustachioed, his thick dark hair glossy as a boot.

By that time Edith had learned much about her headstrong husband which might have given her pause, had she known before their union. Fred was two very different men. One would disappear for weeks at a time without warning, only to return careening drunk, bellowing at the top of his lungs and firing the heavy revolver he invariably carried. When he sobered up he was stricken with remorse, and would turn into the untypical man she had married, helping with the laundry and doing the dishes, menial tasks which most men would not consider performing. Then he would explode again, a pattern of excess followed by remorse.

There was no going back for Edith. She was past the marriageable age, and decent people simply did not divorce, no matter how strong the provocation. Even if the fault was probably the husband's the woman would be blamed. She had no rights; she was a chattel. Women had little place outside the home, and with an infant at the breast Edith was doubly trapped. Fred did provide well, but he controlled all the money.

There was one small consolation: Edith had gained a small measure of control over him which no one else exercised. She could calm his furies, and she learned to cope with them.

Their second child, a son, was born in 1902, and they named him Charles Fred. In 1904 Edith inherited the farms. A U.S. Patent issued to "Edith J. Frye, formerly Edith J. Bronson" was registered in the Rolette County land registry office on December 1 that year.

Edith was pregnant again the next spring when they traveled by rail to Montana to visit her sisters and father. They left behind a half-finished barn and a framed-in house, intending to return in time for spring planting.

Julius Abraham Bronson, tall, long-legged and thin, was a vigorous man. There was much talk in the territory about new lands in Canada being opened up by the railways. The Grand Trunk was due to reach Edmonton within the year, and would eventually traverse a pass called the Yellowhead. Fred and his father-in-law rode north to explore the country beyond the railhead while Edith returned home to North Dakota with the children.

While Edith worked alongside the carpenters to finish the house and barn, Fred and his father-in-law fought their way through the swamps and muskegs west of Edmonton and spent an entire season exploring the mountain ranges beyond the Yellowhead Pass. On the way back they had to kill a horse for food at a place on the Fraser River called Tete Jaune Cache, where trappers used to store their furs before taking them to trade at Jasper House, a hundred miles east.

The railroads were busy in North Dakota that year. The "Soo Line", the Minneapolis, St. Paul and Sault Ste. Marie Railway, built a long branch line running east-west through the state's northern counties, while the Great Northern constructed a number of branches that intersected the Soo Line at intervals. When the Soo Line secured control of the land at the crossing of their line and the Great Northern's it established the town of Rolette at that intersection. The GN retaliated by starting McCumber as a rival town about two miles to the north.

When Fred returned home that fall Edith presented him with a second daughter, Frances. The house and barn were completed, the crop harvested, but Fred paid little attention. He was determined they would make their fortune by getting in on the railroad construction in Canada. It would be years before the railroads would announce construction plans though, and Edith had no wish to leave the farm she loved for some unexplored wilderness. Fred agreed to bide his time and turned his attention to the business at hand. In mid-November, the *McCumber Herald* announced,

> Otto A. Olson disposed of his livery stable last week, in exchange for a fine quarter of a section of land, several miles south of town. The new proprietor is Fred Frye, who expects to erect an additional building to better handle the increasing business. Mr. Frye retains the services of L.A. Graham and two other employees are Walter and Louis Taylor. Fred Schroeder has left the barn but is still in the employ of Mr. Olson.

The next week, the *Herald* announced,

> The *Herald* is informed that Fred Frye, the new proprietor of the livery stable, will build a 30x80 addition to his establishment.

On Thursday, December 14, the newspaper proclaimed,

> Fred Frye has purchased some fine halters and harness for his livery business and he is well-equipped to serve the public.

Undaunted by the onslaught of winter, Fred began construction. The *Herald* of Thursday, January 18, 1906, recorded,

> Fred Frye has been making good progress with the building of his livery barn, considering the unfavorable weather this week. The new building is 30x80 feet, 16 feet posts, and with the building in use at present the size of the

barn on the ground floor will be 54x80. The front part of the barn, 24x50 feet, will be used for a carriage room.

The next week the paper stated,

> Fred Frye's new livery barn is looming up and filling a lot of space. It will be a substantial improvement to the town.

Buying and improving the livery business was proving to be an expensive undertaking. However, getting ready cash was no problem for a man of Fred's resources. A single trip to Montana and he would return flush with money, after having disposed of a cargo of illicit whisky. The Thursday, April 5, *McCumber Herald* noted,

> Fred Frye returned Sunday afternoon from a business trip nearly as far as Havre, Mont. On his return Mr. Frye came by team from Rugby, accompanied by Fred Stokey of that village.

While Fred was busy with the livery business and his bootlegging, Edith had her hands full running the farm. In May the *Herald* reported,

> Fred Frye is keeping bachelor hall, his family having gone to the farm to remain during the seeding season.

Unchecked by Edith's presence, Fred easily fell into his wild ways.

The Flight

Fred's investment in the livery stable in McCumber had not been a prudent move. Despite the substantial improvements he had made, Rolette, at the intersection of the two railroads, was becoming the better business town. Many disgruntled McCumber businessmen were talking of moving to the rival camp. His failing prospects did Fred Frye's normally bad temper no good, and he was feeling quarrelsome when he and an acquaintance named Bert Reynolds set out before dawn in Fred's wagon for the train depot at Rugby some time in May, 1906.

Some distance from McCumber, Fred turned off the main road and followed a twisting lane between thick willows. He pulled up the team beside the sagging remains of a sod house dug into the hillside. Fred heaved a heavy folded canvas tarp out of the wagonbox while Reynolds climbed down and went into the abandoned hovel.

Reynolds came out carrying a wooden crate filled with bottles. It clinked as he heaved it up with an effort. Fred took the crate easily and set it down in the wagonbox. He pulled the staples out to drop the tailgate and went back to the box. He pulled one bottle out and held it to the moonlight. It was full to the shoulder. So were the others. Without comment, he slid them all back and jammed the cushioning straw back into the crate. Reynolds carried out another crate and Frye checked that one, too. They did not talk.

Within half an hour the wagon was loaded with a layer of crates full of long-necked bottles and quart canning jars. Frye sat on the tailgate, legs swinging, and spun the rim off a Mason jar. He spilled a few drops onto the iron chain of the tailgate and struck a match with his thumbnail. The liquid sputtered and fizzled and the match went out.

"Wouldn't do to sell spoiled goods," Frye said ambiguously. He tipped his head back and took a long draught, his Adam's apple working up and down.

"Like a snort?" He offered the jar, an impressive two inches lower.

Reynolds drank and coughed as the raw spirit burned his throat and seared his sinuses. He did not see Frye slide the short-barreled Colt from his waistband and lay it beside his leg, cocking it silently.

"Powerful stuff," Reynolds croaked when he had his voice back.

"Not so powerful as it ought to be," Frye said. "Where's the rest of it?"

Reynolds stared up at him. "Count 'em yourself. There's forty cases there, ever' last one."

"And every one's short. There's an inch off the top of each jug and it's been watered. I may do a lot of things but I don't water my liquor."

Frye felt very light, his senses clear and keen. The rounded butt of the Colt was hard against his palm. Reynolds brushed back his coat and fumbled for a gun. Frye lifted the heavy revolver and fired, the barrel nearly touching the chest of the other man. The soft lead slug drove Reynolds into the hole that was the door of the old sod house. Frye threw himself off the tailgate, lying flat behind the wheel and fired again, aiming carefully. The body jerked at the second impact but did not move.

Frye waited two minutes, the sound of the shots ringing in his ears, his heart beating against the damp hard ground. When he was sure, he approached from one side, revolver cocked. Reynolds was dead, the front of his shirt burned by the first shot, his chest a matted red mess.

The gunfire had not made much noise outside the copse. Climbing the knoll behind the sod house, Frye could see nothing moving in the dim light before true dawn.

Back in the hollow he lifted Reynolds' body easily, holding it away from himself, and carried it twenty yards to a half collapsed root cellar in the crumbling bank. A hole in the soil above the door showed where earth had fallen in between the timbers. He thrust the body into the hole, then returned with a short spade and broke more dirt into the cavity. The steep bank would spill more soil down with the spring rains, and the summer heat would bake the clay adobe-hard.

Reynolds' revolver was lying inside the door of the dugout. Frye unloaded it, then flung it far into the thick brush. He tied the tarp over the crates, backed and turned the wagon and drove slowly off. Reynolds had disappeared from the face of the earth. The thin light of dawn spread across the horizon, and the full moon hovered above the far-off hills, brighter than the sun.

Frye reached Rugby two hours later and turned off the main street to follow a lane beside a railroad spur which led to an abattoir. He backed the wagon up to a loading dock where several men wearing bloodstained aprons and high rubber boots were waiting.

"You're late," grumbled a red-faced man with a large, hard paunch. "Should've been here before daylight!"

"Had to fix a rim," Frye said, climbing back and untying the tarp. He began handing the crates out.

They were taken swiftly into the slaughterhouse, where rows of hog carcasses swung on iron hooks. It was cold inside. Sawdust stained by meat juices covered the floor.

The men broke the crates open and stuffed the jars and bottles into the body cavities of the hogs. One took

24

an awl and thick hemp twine and laced the lips of the bellies together. The first carcass stuffed with moonshine was carried into a waiting boxcar loaded with ice even before the last crate was unloaded.

Frye handed the plant foreman a wad of dollar bills and received a sheaf of bills of lading in return. He drove the empty wagon to a livery stable where the owner came out and took the team. Frye pulled his Gladstone from beneath the seat and nearly froze. Reynolds' ragged carpetbag lay beside it. He pulled it out, too, and dropped to the ground holding both bags.

He was sweating in the cold as he walked down the street to the train depot and bought a single Pullman ticket. His sixth sense of impending danger was vibrating; his collar rasped like hemp against the stubble of his neck.

"What takes you out west, Mr. Frye?" asked the agent, writing out the ticket.

"Business," Frye said, laying his finger beside his nose.

The agent laughed knowingly and slid the ticket beneath the wicket. Frye took both bags out onto the platform. The train was waiting, the locomotive panting beneath the watering tank. The conductor punched his ticket and indicated a car.

"Middle compartment, left, Mr. Frye."

Frye nodded and climbed aboard. Once in the compartment he locked the door and ripped open the carpetbag. It was shabby and worn, no match for his expensive Gladstone. There was little inside: a change of collars, a razor, a harmonica in a tattered cardboard case, a woolen coat and a pair of shoelaces.

He laid the bag aside, lit a cigar and sat far back so he could see out without being seen. The bills of lading crackled in his breast pocket. He began to think, coldly and clearly.

Reynolds' bag was a death warrant if it was discovered in his possession. No one had remarked on it, though. If he disembarked in Butte without the old bag it was unlikely that anyone would notice. The window of the Pullman opened, though it was usually shut against the smoke and cinders from the engine. He could heave the bag out at the first river they crossed. The bag would float, though, unless there was something heavy in it. There was a porcelain-covered iron pitcher above the basin in the Pullman. He could fill that with water and it would carry the carpetbag down.

The body was well hidden. He had removed all traces of the still he had operated there, all except the clay firebox. The wooded brake was well away from any habitation, and not on the usual route he would have taken from McCumber. No one had seen him and Reynolds leave the town in the dead of night.

The train lurched and began to back. The depot slid aside as if it were moving and not the train. The cigar had gone out. Frye lit another match and puffed the rich leaf back to life.

Did the man have any close friends? Family? He had been a bachelor, and his accent was southern.

The train clashed to a halt. There was a pause while the boxcar was coupled, and then the train began to move forward. The steam whistle blew; the wheels began to play a rhythm over the tracks.

Frye slid open the window and peered out. The train was moving at a good clip now, faster than any horse could run. A narrow bridge was coming up. He filled the pitcher from the tiny tap, wadded a sleeve of the coat to keep it from spilling and stuffed it into the carpetbag. A blast of cinders blew into the window, obscuring all vision on that side of the train. The clacking of the wheels turned to a hollow rumble as the train crossed the bridge. Frye heaved the bag well out and slammed the window shut.

The conductor passed down the corridor, calling out for breakfast. Frye wet his handkerchief at the tap, wiped his face clean of smut and cinders and went out to breakfast, locking the door of the compartment behind him.

It was time to move on. His string had run out in North Dakota. Canada beckoned.

High wagons crawled across the fields of the Frye farms two months later, drawing early sun-cured stooks to the ricks, rising like great tawny loaves beside the barn.

Harems of black Minorca chickens guarded by their roosters scratched and pecked among the newly-cut stubble. Hawks hovered above the mowers far out in the fields, waiting for prey to be flushed by the clacking blades. A farm hand standing on a mound of hay atop a horse-drawn wagon forked golden sheaves into the barn loft.

Edith, nauseated by the heat and another pregnancy, looked out over the farm she had cherished and wondered for the thousandth time when her will-o'-the-wisp husband would ever return. Bloody rumors about the disappearance of Reynolds had begun to spread and Fred had fled to Seattle in June, leaving Edith to sell the farm and stock and pack for Canada. They would travel in the big freight wagons, taking everything they owned with them. Edith had readily found a buyer, one Richard N. Widmeyer. The consideration was $5,500, a very good price. The sale was recorded in July.

Fred had arranged to sell the livery business back to Olson. The June 28 *Herald* reported,

> Otto A. Olson is again in the livery business and is ready to meet the needs of the public in that line. Mr. Frye has retired from the business.

All was chaos inside the farmhouse that stood like a giant crackerbox on the treeless prairie. Packing crates and litter crowded the wide back porch. It was hot in the kitchen and flies buzzed on the ceiling. Edith had sorted and discarded, carefully packing the clothes the children had outgrown. There would be other children born in the wilderness, and no stores.

Out in the farmyard five-year-old Myrtle was tending the fire beneath a twenty-gallon iron kettle for boiling clothes. Baby Frances, barely a year old, was napping on the shaded porch in a wicker bassinet covered with cheesecloth to keep off the flies. Myrtle, a determined and serious little girl, bossed three-year-old Charles like a little mother as he dragged up stovewood.

Edith husked her hands together, feeling the callouses, the harsh fruit of thousands of hours of labor: hoeing, digging fencepost holes, stringing barbed wire, roping, branding. A tiny spider crawled down the wall and she flicked it off, automatically.

"Bad luck," she thought, and turned back to the stench of the diapers waiting to be scrubbed.

Edith had long since washed and wiped the dishes, scrubbed the children's faces and tucked them in. She had nursed the baby to sleep and finally gone to bed. Dusk fell late but it was dark when she was awakened by the pop-pop-pop of gunfire and the rush and thunder of a horse. Fred was home, raving drunk.

The sound of heavy boots shuddered the house. Her bedroom door crashed open and Fred stumbled in, reeking of whisky and horses. He grabbed Edith's arm and pulled her out of bed, overturning the bedside table. The coal-oil lamp shattered on the floor and the pungent odor of kerosene flooded the room.

Fred slipped and fell, cursing. Something hot and wet splattered Edith's face. She found the matchbox, struck a match and gasped. Fred sprawled splay-legged among the shards of the brittle lamp chimney clutching his left arm. Bright arterial blood pumped from his thick wrist.

"Cut m'self," he slurred, drunkenly.

Edith pulled him to his feet and shuffling through the broken glass half carried him downstairs to the kitchen. She sat him in a chair, ripped his sleeve to make a tourniquet and twisted the band tight. The bleeding slowed. She laid a scoop of flour in a dishcloth, rolled it into a cylinder, then drew out the razor-edged shard from his wrist. She bound the dishcloth over the wound, then loosened the tourniquet. The bulky bandage reddened immediately, but after a few minutes the bleeding slowed. Edith guided her drunken husband to a daybed and lowered him on it, laying his injured arm on a chair by his side.

Dawn was breaking by the time she swept up the broken glass, mopped the blood trail through the house and put the blood-speckled sheets into the laundry tub to soak. Fred snored loudly on the day couch. Edith checked him frequently to be sure he did not toss and open the wound. She had fed the children and shooed them outside long before he awakened.

Fred appeared in mid-morning like an apparition, his face drawn and pale from the loss of blood, his arm wrapped in the clotted bandage, blackened blood staining his hand. Edith had no inhibitions against confronting him in his weakened condition.

"I don't know why I do this for you," she said, cutting the bandage away gingerly. "Seems like you'll never learn to leave that rotgut alone. I should have just left that tourniquet off last night and let you bleed to death. You don't care what you're doing to your family!"

Fred accepted her rebuke contritely, and in the following days was a changed man. The gash in his arm healed quickly, leaving only a thin white scar that did not tan, and no disability.

Homestead fever was sweeping the country. A number of families in Rolette and surrounding counties were picking up stakes and heading for Canada. Fred, an acknowledged leader and resourceful guide who had been in Canada before, was elected the captain of a train of some twenty wagons.

Fred threw himself into the task of organizing the trek. He culled their stock, keeping only the fittest cattle, inspected the big boat-bodied Concorde freight wagons and repaired the harness of the four horse teams. Each wagon carried a heavy canvas cover stretched over thick bows made of saplings bolted to the wagon boxes. The ends could be opened or closed by flaps against the weather. He spent two days trimming the Clydesdales' hooves and shoeing them. When that was accomplished he heaved the steel-faced iron anvil and the cast iron forge into the heaviest wagon, which he would drive. He dismounted the iron wheels of the mower and the hay rake and slid them into his wagon. Spare wheels, extra axles, harness and harness leather, grease, grindstone, wheat grinder, rope, block and tackle, chains, crosscut saws, axes and extra handles, shovels, mattocks, picks and adzes were checked and double-checked. For months to come they would be a mobile, self-sufficient society. Anything they had not brought with them they would have to do without.

When nearly all was ready, Edith surveyed the

wagons.

"Where are you going to put my stove?" she asked.

Fred gaped. "You're not going to take that! Weighs near a ton!"

"Oh, yes I am," Edith said. "My mother left me that stove. I'm not going to cook on a camp stove ever again."

"Well, I married you for your cooking," Fred sighed. "We'll take it."

He uncoupled the gleaming woodstove with its bright nickel trim, cursing the shower of soot, and wrestled it up gangplanks into the wagon Edith would drive. He bolted the feet down and vented the stovepipe through an asbestos patch Edith sewed into the canvas. Beside the stove he drove a line of nails to hang her pots and pans, and on the other side installed a forty-gallon water barrel. The churn stood beside the water barrel, held upright by a leather strap. The motion of the wagon would do much of the churning.

The children would ride with Edith and sleep next to the warm stove. The barnyard stock would ride in Fred's wagon, the poultry in crates. Hired drovers would drive the cattle.

By August all was ready. With a volley of shots and shouted good-byes to the neighbors who gathered to see them off, the wagon train lurched north toward Winnipeg in the rutted trough of the old cattle trail.

Edith slapped the reins and her team leaned into the traces, sending the milk in the churn slapping and sloshing. With Charles and Myrtle on the hard high seat beside her and the baby in the cradle lashed behind, a piece of jerky tied to her wrist by a string, Edith left her childhood home behind.

Within a year McCumber would literally vanish, most of the buildings moved to Rolette. The townsite returned to prairie.

Trekking West

The cattle trail wound northeast, following the contours of the land. The herd of mixed dairy and beef cattle walked in lines behind the wagons. The outriders covered their noses and mouths with bandanas against the choking dust. Their clothing was soon stained the color of prairie soil.

The dust was thick enough to choke in the wagons. From necessity, the wagoneers spaced themselves far enough apart to let the wind blow most of the dust from the next wagon aside. That precluded conversation; they were too far apart to shout. The children could run from one wagon to another, but the drivers were isolated on their jolting platforms.

Clouds of carnivorous flies made the teams tetchy despite the horse nets that helped to keep their heads protected. A scum of dust settled across the milk in the churn, the water barrel, the pots and pans, and seeped into everything. Myrtle sneezed through the handkerchief tied across her face. Charles was asleep, his red bandana clotted to his face with dust and sweat.

The plain was a series of shallow basins, their lips often gravelly. Good wild hay sometimes grew in the marshy centers of the bowls but there was little water. A few ponds fringed with cottonwood and willows pooled beside the trail, but most were alkaline and showed white salts around the edges. These pools were good for washing clothes but the stock would not drink from them. Sometimes two shallow lakes would be connected by a narrow, meandering neck. The lower lake would be bitter but the upper which drained into it, sweet. The lakes abounded in ducks, loons, yellowlegs and snipe, and the boom of shotguns echoed across the ponds in the evenings after camp had been made.

They were more than a week out when they came to the first sizable river. Fred crossed first, his big bay mare, Judy, tethered behind his wagon. Edith followed Fred over the ford. The high wheels of her wagon barely touched bottom in the centre of the river. Behind her one of the other wagoneers, a widower named Brown, drove his wagon down the sloping bank downstream from where Fred had crossed.

"Brown!" bellowed Fred from the far shore. "Not there! You're going to miss the ford!"

Brown's team, feeling the bottom drop from beneath their hooves and with inexperienced hands at the reins, turned downstream with the current. The water rose over the wagon wheels and the off horse panicked, snorting and squealing. Brown hauled on the reins at the horses tried to turn back, plunging in the harness.

"Give 'em their head!" Fred screamed.

He jerked Judy's reins loose and heaved himself into the saddle, shaking out his lariat as he headed downstream. The willows lining the bank were thick but he drove the horse through them, keeping his head lowered against the branches which slashed at his face.

Brown's wagon lifted and lurched as one wheel scraped over a boulder. The load shifted and the upstream wheels came out of the water. Brown pitched into the tangle of harness as his wagon capsized and rolled, pulling the screaming horses under. The drovers tried to pace the wagon through the thick brush lining the banks but were quickly outdistanced by the remorseless current.

Too late to put a line on the wreck, Fred turned and urged the long-legged mare back to the ford. The other wagons had halted until Fred could return.

"We'll line them all over," he told the shocked assembly.

They tied ropes to the rear of the wagons to keep them from drifting and all made the ford without further incident. The cattle came up then, the drovers behind, popping their ropes. The cattle stampeded into the brush on the far side and it was hours before the cowhands could round them up and get them lined out again. The wagons were late in making camp, in a patch of first a couple of miles beyond the ford. Two head of cattle had been lost, drowned when others climbed up over them to get to dry land. It was a somber camp.

The next day they searched the river for the wagon, without success. Brown had been swallowed by the river. Letters explaining the incident were written and a drover sent back to report the tragedy.

The promise of a clear day lifted their spirits somewhat the next morning and the horror of the drowning seemed to diminish. They started away from the river as soon as possible.

By noon the sky to the west was fleeced over with billowing white clouds, and before them was a swollen black cloud. A dun-colored mass of cloud flickering with lightning extended to the north and pillars of rain crossed the prairie.

The wind struck with the ferocity of a tornado, so hard that the horses were turned off the track, away from the wind. Hail and rain crackled down on the canvas. The line of the caravan was broken. Fred stood up on his wagon seat and pointed to a nearby spruce grove. His shout was lost in the wind but all the wagons turned and fled before the onslaught of the storm to the shelter of the trees. The cattle milled behind.

The torrential rains turned the prairie into a red gumbo. The wagon wheels picked up huge slabs of clay that built up then peeled off the iron rims.

All through the rest of August and the hot month of

September they crawled north. The women were becoming accustomed to driving the heavy wagons and often spelled the men. The children would run alongside the wagons until they tired, then would climb up.

For weeks they traveled on level ground, broken by an occasional ravine or small gully, and the wagons made good time. The women washed diapers nightly if there was any water available.

The terrain grew more rugged as they inched northwest, breaking off from the old cattle trail. They began to encounter heavily wooded valleys between tall grassy hills. Their progress slowed to only a few miles a day, and the men had to go ahead with axes and saws to clear a trail, leaving most of the driving to the women.

In the valleys lay basins of thick black loam surrounding ponds. The wagons sank nearly to their axles in the muck, jolting over hidden roots and boulders. When especially difficult stretches were encountered they would camp for two or three days while the men built a road.

The weather grew chilly as October closed and the night watch donned winter coats. As if in compensation for the cold the insects and much of the choking dust disappeared.

November was upon them when the wagon train emerged from a low pass into a broad valley enclosed by wooded hills above a wall of rimrock. A small stream wandered through thick wild hay waist-high to a tall man. Thick firs offered shelter for the stock, timber for cabins and shakes, and firewood. At either end the valley narrowed, and the drovers easily threw up brush fences to keep the stock from wandering. With all hands free to wield axes and saws, a small settlement quickly rose. Well before Christmas they were ready for winter.

Time dragged in the tiny community. The men hunted or trapped, but the women were tied to the cabins by the children and the burdens of cooking and laundering. Food gathering was practically their only entertainment. High-bush cranberries with tart, wizened fruit grew thickly along the stream.

When the weather grew poor, they opened a school in one of the cabins. Christmas passed, and the January wind hissed over the roofs, spitting pellets of hard snow. By February, Edith could feel the baby moving inside. March passed, and the warm April rains churned the frozen ground to mud. The wagons started out again on the last lap for Moose Jaw.

The heavily laden Concordes cut deep ruts, and the Clydesdales' hairy fetlocks turned into cumbersome balls of clinging mud that tired the horses. The drovers huddled in thick oilskins over lap robes, balaclava helmets pulled down over their ears. The wind beat on the stuff canvas of the wagons.

The creeks were swollen by the freshet. Groves of aspen, balsam, poplar and birch lined the banks. Clumps of aspen on small, flooded islets were bent in the current.

They came into a much larger valley than any they had encountered before. A sizable river bordered by greening meadows ran down the valley in great swooping loops. They were all eager for a change in diet after the monotonous menu over the winter. At one camp Edith got out her fishing pole and baited a large hook with a piece of venison. Her hook had no sooner hit the water than she had a heavy strike. The thick bamboo rod bent and the line, wound around the tip, stripped off. A huge fish thrashed in the current. Edith dug her heels in but felt her grip slipping.

"Fred!" she yelled. "It's pulling me in!"

Fred jogged up and took the pole from her, laughing. He fought the fish for several minutes until it tired, then heaved a monster Dolly Varden char flopping onto the bank. Edith was on it in a second with a branch.

"Don't beat it to a pulp!" Fred admonished. "Hit it on the head and kill it!"

The big fish was nearly two feet long and weighed better than ten pounds, they figured. Its sides held bright streaks of color. The name Dolly Varden came from the dress, cut in the Wateau style with a deep cleavage and a bright skirt. From then on, they fished every night at the camp.

The valley deepened as they traveled and they were forced to track along steep sidehills when the river threw loops across their path. At last, they reached a point where the river cut deep under a sheer, crumbling bluff, and there was no way to proceed except by fording the river.

Fred untied his mare from behind the wagon and rode gingerly down the bank, turning this way and that, testing the footing. At river's edge the tall horse sank to its knees and rolled, throwing Fred into the swift current. Edith pulled out the lariat she kept underneath her wagon seat in case she ever needed to trip a runaway team and shook a loop free. She ran to the riverbank and swung the rope out but missed Fred. Flailing against the current, he splashed out of sight around the bend.

Edith quickly drew in the rope. Whirling it once more, she dropped the loop over the mare's neck and ran back to tie the end to the wagon tree. Grasping the big Clydes by their bridles she forced them back. The rope became taut and the mare stumbled out onto firm ground, blowing and trembling. Edith was about to climb into the saddle when a halloo came from around the bend.

Fred, dripping wet, came up on a horse behind one of the drovers. He slid off in front of Edith.

"Guess I've had my spring bath," he puffed, shivering and blowing. "Like it a bit warmer, though."

The drover coiled his damp rope and tied it back to the saddlehorn. "I figured it was a calf or something valuable so I dropped a rope on it and let it drift to shore," he joked.

They made camp while Fred decided what to do. They now knew the river was too fast above the big bluff to ford. They would have to find a way around it, or else backtrack for days or weeks to find a suitable ford. In the end, he decided to find a route out of the valley. Most of the men went off with a team of workhorses, a scraper and a grader to clear the road. The women settled down to wait their return in a number of days.

The camp stood nearly deserted. Most of the women were washing clothes at the river, the children fishing or playing nearby. Edith dozed, cocoon-warm inside a quilt on her wagonseat, the sun beating on her eyelids. The beat of a hammer on an iron rim and the muted chuck of axes far-off blended in a lulling percussion.

Suddenly a tiny spark of alarm interrupted her formless dreams. A woman's voice rose, then stopped abruptly. Edith sat up and listened hard, her heart pounding. The sudden silence beat as loudly as her pulse.

Two of the men who had remained were running toward the river. Edith half turned and lifted the long Winchester from its pegs behind the wagon seat. There was a hubbub of voices and the women came hurrying back from the river, herding the children before them.

"What is it?" Edith called.

One of the women, grim-faced, shook her head.

Another grouped the children by the wagons. "Now you stay put. Any one of you who strays ten feet from the wagons is going to get a licking so you won't be able to sit for a week!"

"What is it?" Edith asked again.

"Mrs. McLeod has been attacked," said the first woman, grimly. "Luckily the men came on them."

"Who was it?"

"That drover, you know, the one who joined at the last minute. Swede, they call him."

"What are they going to do?" Edith asked.

"Hang him, probably." The woman laughed without humor. "Better than he deserves."

A rider was sent to fetch back Fred and the working party. In a grove of trees, well segregated from the wagons, a brief drumhead court-martial was held. None of the women attended the trial.

Late in the evening the men came trooping back, grim-faced, without the drover who had assaulted the woman. He had been hanged on a convenient tree, and buried in a shallow grave.

The children, for once, were abashed, and slunk obediently to bed while the men gathered around the central campfire. A bottle of whisky made the rounds while the men talked quietly. Edith and several of the women sat up late, knitting. There was considerable speculation whether the man had been encouraged.

Fred came to bed, late. "We'll put her off at the first town," he told Edith, quietly. "And no one will say anything."

"I just don't know, Fred," Edith replied. "This is a terrible thing. It's going to change everything. I just want to get away from here. I'm a good enough teamster on level ground but I don't know what I'd do if the team slipped and started sliding back on the mountain we have to climb to get out of here. It takes more strength than I have to make that brake work. But I don't want to stay here any longer; not a day! This place is haunted."

The rest of them were of a similar mind. They hitched up the next morning and moved the wagons upriver, out of sight of the great bluff that stood like a headstone above the death camp.

The wagon train gradually returned to normal. The adults never mentioned the hanging to the children, although some of the older ones figured out what had taken place and told the younger children. However, they learned never to mention the matter within the hearing of an adult.

Edith could no longer climb in and out of her wagon except with great difficulty. The road builders were due back almost any day when regular contractions began. Her wagon was cleared, clean sheets were made ready, and early one morning the squall of a baby girl split the air.

When Fred and the work crew returned, Edith greeted him with his newest daughter.

"I've decided to name her Ella," she said.

The baby was fat and healthy, and Edith doted on her; she was a symbol, almost, of a new life in the wilderness. She knew, though, that Fred would have been more pleased by a boy. Sons were a sign of a man's virility, it was commonly believed.

The trail back to the new road out of the valley was marked by their earlier passage, and they made good time. A line of blazes led away from the river, up an even gully formed by a small creek. There was room for two wagons to travel side by side but Fred ordered that they go single file.

They double-teamed the horses and fixed crude but effective brakes by chaining a log behind the rear wheels, parallel to the axle. If the team slipped and the wagon rolled back, it could jam to a stop against the log.

With two teams of horses hauling each wagon, the Concordes creaked and groaned up the steep slope. At the top of the ridge they blocked the wagons and rode the teams down to bring the next one up.

A stiff wind crested the height of land, pushing the mosquitoes back. For miles on end the country unrolled, meadows above, timber below and winding streams in the valleys. The emerging leaves colored the foliage a delicate green. They had reached the border of the promised land, it seemed, and they sat watching until sunset.

"We can make good here, I know it," Fred told Edith. "We can get in on the ground floor."

Edith turned to face him. "I know we can. I feel so much better now, with the new baby and all." She kept to herself any dark thoughts. Perhaps with enough of a challenge to occupy him, Fred could control his drinking.

The anguished bellow of a calf and the banshee shriek of a cougar sheared the air late that night. Shrill neighing echoed through the valley, mixed with the bawling of cattle. The ground trembled as the herd stampeded down from the rim toward the unexplored valley.

The men jammed their boots on and ran for their horses. Edith and the other women rose and kindled the fires. It was dangerous work; anything could happen to a rider at night, on unfamiliar ground. A horse could stumble and throw its rider; a branch could poke an eye out. There was no choice but to pursue the cattle, though; everyone had too much money tied up in the stock.

It was late the next day before all the riders returned. They were scratched and bush-whipped, their faces swollen with insect bites. The horses were lathered and stumbling. Nearly half the herd had stampeded, and there was little hope of finding all of them with the few riders they had.

They brought the wagons down the grade, dragging logs behind as brakes, and lined out again at the bottom. As they progressed they found more of the cattle, which docilely rejoined the herd.

The wagon train entered open prairie again and turned almost due west. The country varied from a sandy loam to a deep black peat. Occasionally, they encountered ridges of overgrown sand dunes blown in from the north.

They passed Fort Ellice at the junction of the Qu'Appelle and Assiniboine Rivers. The collection of white buildings twinkled on a plateau two hundred feet above the rivers. The streams, emerging from their long valleys, ran so slowly that their united water ran through the intervale in great lazy loops. The rivers slid around islands, some soft and grassy, thick with waterfowl; others covered with willow and timber.

Several days later they reached their destination, Moose Jaw, a sizable city by that time. It was past midsummer.

Bearberry

After he had found Edith comfortable housing near Moose Jaw where she could look after the stock, Fred took a packtrain west with a hired hand named Roy Loucks. Loucks' wife Helen and their children lived nearby, and Edith and Helen Loucks became fast friends.

In the late fall, Roy Loucks returned, alone. Fred had gone ahead to guide a crew of railroad surveyors through the mountains to a place called Kamloops. Edith resigned herself, and when the Arctic winds whipped the snow into great drifts, she knew he would not return before spring.

Rain drizzled down the panes that spring of 1908 and beat the yard into a morass of mud. Edith looked out to see a wedge of Canada Geese honking overhead as they swept north, and saw Fred on his bay mare turn in at the gate. Fred was so dirty, travel-worn and ragged that Edith hardly recognized him.

"Well, aren't you glad to see me?" Fred asked, pitching his hat into the sitting room and taking Edith in his arms.

She turned away, angrily. "Where have you been all

this time? The children were expecting you for Christmas! They need a father, sometimes!"

"Don't you worry about that!" Fred pulled out a thick wad of bills and tossed it onto a table. "We had potatoes and moose meat for Christmas, and darn glad to get it. We slept out without tents, but we were making good wages, at least."

He and another man named Dave Henry were offered high wages to guide a party of surveyors and engineers over the Yellowhead Pass and down the North Thompson River valley to Kamloops. Along the way they paused for a night at Camp Creek, some forty miles south of Tete Jaune Cache, on the summit between the Fraser and Columbia watersheds. By coincidence, Sanford Fleming on his railroad survey expedition of 1872 had camped at the same spot. The valley there was narrow, and any railroad which was built through the valley would pass nearby. It was ideal for what Fred had in mind, and he filed it away as a potential homestead. After guiding the party to Kamloops, Fred returned to Camp Creek with a trapping outfit and spent the winter harvesting the abundant beaver.

The Canadian Northern had reached Edmonton by 1908, and the Grand Trunk was building fast behind, due to arrive in another year or so. The Fryes would need to be further west if they were to get in on the railroad boom, and Fred would not wait any longer at Moose Jaw. They could travel via Canadian Pacific from Moose Jaw to a place called Red Deer, traveling "settlers' effects" in boxcars.

There had been a considerable increase in Edith's stock since their arrival, and she boasted nearly a hundred Black Minorca chickens as well. The winter had been profitable for her. They culled the cattle, keeping the best breeding stock, and drove them into holding pens beside the railroad. The big Concorde wagons were rolled onto the flatcars, jacked up, the wheels removed and chained down. The wagons' canvas tops were collapsed and lashed tight over the boxes.

They rolled out of Moose Jaw with their legs dangling out of the boxcar doors, while Edith fretted about the children's safety. For two days and nights the countryside rolled by. Periodically, the train stopped to allow the Fryes to feed and water the cattle. During the brief halts Edith kindled small fires by the roadbed and cooked hot meals. The rest of the time they ate cold food, as railroad regulations forbade lighting campstoves in the boxcars. At Red Deer they disembarked and camped near the railroad stockyards until they could move out onto the prairie where forage was available.

Edith camped in the wagons near Red Deer to look after the cattle, while Fred and Roy Loucks rode north to Edmonton where jobs freighting for the railroad were said to be available. Again, Roy returned alone, and this time not because Fred had found a job. He was in jail.

Fred had been sentenced to a month for his part in a barroom brawl in which several men had been badly injured. In the meantime, Roy Loucks had secured a contract for freighting and needed to buy more horses and wagons. In a day he was gone, taking the two big freight wagons with him.

There was a fair wagon road south from Red Deer, so Edith took her light wagon and spent a day driving around the country. She settled on a farm of about a hundred acres with considerable grazing rights near Bearberry. She returned to Red Deer with the deed in her pocket. In a month she was settled in the nicest house she had known. With money left over from the sale of the farms in North Dakota she bought complete winter outfits for herself and the children, the first she had had since her marriage.

Fred returned from jail looking pale but clear-eyed and rested. He was anxious to go back north to start freighting, but Edith put her foot down.

"Oh no you don't," she told him. "You've left me and the kids alone too much already. I'm tired of being a grass widow. You've got to take time to be a father, and there's a hundred things around here I want you to do. Roy has done just fine with the freighting so far, and you can afford to spend some time right here."

For the next few weeks Fred settled down into the domestic routine and accomplished an amount of work that would have taken most men twice the time. He had been home a month when Roy Loucks rode into the yard on a saddlehorse.

Edith watched from the house as Fred saddled up and rode off with Loucks, thinking he would be home later in the day. When he did not return the next day or the next, she began to worry. She harnessed up her team and drove to see the horse trader with whom Fred had been dealing for more wagon teams.

"Why, they said they was going direct to Edmonton," the man told Edith.

Edith returned to the ranch, humiliated and furious. She would not see her husband again for nearly five months, by which time she was two thirds through another pregnancy.

Edith found her new ranch ideal for raising cattle. The railroad construction nearing Edmonton boosted cattle prices, and she invested in more stock. Fred was home infrequently. He was absent when Edith delivered another daughter, Lottie, in 1909.

In the meantime, plans were going ahead for the new railroads. Late in 1908, Mackenzie and Mann, the partners who controlled the Canadian Northern Railway, had received a number of invitations from the British Columbia government to discuss extension of the line. Premier McBride, the newspapers revealed, saw the need for transportation to open up the province's resources and at the same time provide tax revenues to transform chronic provincial deficits into surpluses.

In January of 1909, Premier McBride announced that British Columbia would soon have another rail connection with the prairies. Fred was hauling freight out of Edmonton, and Edith learned from the newspapers that the negotiations were with Mackenzie and Mann.

Swinging around the bottom of Beaverhill Lake and cutting through the Beaver Hills, the Grand Trunk Pacific reached Edmonton on August 13, heading for a new port on the Pacific called Prince Rupert. After traversing the Yellowhead Pass, it would follow the upper Fraser, Nechako, Endako and finally the Skeena River valleys to salt water. Fred was making good money hauling freight for the Grand Trunk, with a profitable sideline in moonshine. He was also drinking heavily; whisky was as much a staple for the teamsters as oats for the teams.

There was little more word on the Canadian Northern project until October 19, the day after the dissolution of the British Columbia legislature. Premier McBride, facing cabinet opposition to his support for provincial backing for the railroad, had waited until an election was called before announcing that a contract had in fact been signed with Mackenzie and Mann, providing substantial assistance. In the face of an election there was little criticism of McBride by other Conservatives, and Mc-Bride won all but four seats in the Legislature.

Immediately after the election, the formal agreement between the Canadian Northern Railway and the British Columbia Government was negotiated. The Canadian Northern Pacific Railway was incorporated on January 17, 1910, with authority to construct and operate a railway from the eastern boundary of the province near the Yellowhead Pass, by way of the North Thompson River to Kamloops. From there it would parallel the Canadian Pacific Railway through the Fraser Canyon to the City of New Westminster, then to Vancouver and English Bluff. Legislation enabling the agreement was passed in March. Construction was to begin in July that year, and the entire line was to be completed by July 1, 1914, according to the contract.

Fred planned to take his family almost due north to intercept the railroad right of way near Entwhistle. There was a tote road from there to Fittsue, later called Jasper. They would follow the winter freight route Fred had pioneered through the Drayton Valley, but the frozen lakes and muskegs which were pavements in winter would be treacherous in the thawing spring of the year. Reluctantly, Edith put her beautiful ranch up for sale and prepared to move again.

The first day out, the cattle rebelled against being driven from their accustomed range and stampeded back. A day was lost rounding them up, and Fred hired more cowhands to get them started. By the third day they had got the cattle moving, and kept them on the trot until they settled down. The wagons headed west and north for the dangerous swamps of the Drayton Valley.

Clouds of mosquitoes condensed around the wagons, tormenting the teams. Edith lit a smudge in the stove to smoke the pests out of the wagon, but they suffered as much from the fumes as the pests.

Frequently, they had to detour from Fred's winter route. The men went ahead with axes and saws to slash a narrow road around the lakes. The ax handles became grooved from the thin backs of the crosscut saws. In order to make an undercut to keep windfalls from binding the saws, an ax would be sunk horizontally into the log and the handle used as a fulcrum for the saw. When they had cleared a mile or so, the women would drive the wagons to the end of the slashing, often crossing narrow and treacherous bridges over creeks, or rumbling over corduroy roads laid across the trembling surface of bottomless bogs.

A powerful sulfur odor assaulted their nostrils along the way, and several times they came upon baked, open pans where the ground was too hot to walk. Nearby, gas bubbled through iridescent ponds steaming in the cold air.

Rain swept down at intervals. Brush slapped and scraped the sides of the wagons. Clay gummed the wagon spokes and wheels until they resembled misshapen millstones. The hairy fetlocks of the Clydesdales balled up until they resembled clay stumps. The men were covered with mud from head to toe.

They entered dense spruce swamps and fought through them to the Pembina River, a small stream about a hundred yards wide with poor timber on either side. The freshet had not yet swollen the stream. In the thinning timber the wagons could make better time. Along the banks they could at times see seams of coal.

The sound of a steam whistle on the Grand Trunk shrilled through the swamp late one afternoon as they plodded north. It was not yet dark when the wagons came at last to the freshly cut right of way of the Canadian Northern Railway. Steel had not been laid west of

Edmonton by the Northern, and the Grand Trunk had pushed ahead.

A morain of slashing and boulders lay along the narrow slot cleared through the forest: roots, tree trunks and piles of dirt. Stacks of fresh raw ties rose along both sides of the passage. Edith slapped the reins and the team stumbled out of the swamp and into the fresh slashing. A gang of men hiking back from work dropped their tools and stared, agape at the sight of a small woman driving a freight wagon.

The drovers had a fight on their hands to get the stock to leave the easy, cleared right of way for the swamp that lay between the Canadian Northern and the Grand Trunk lines. Edith could hardly persuade herself to turn the team aside.

Although they could hear the steam whistles from the Grand Trunk, it seemed they would never get through the last rough mile. They had to fight willow and tamarack thickets, swampy meadows and closely set spruce. Night had descended when at last they came out onto the Grand Trunk; a couplet of glistening steel rails on a row of parallel ties curved out of sight into the trees.

The wagons jolted down the debris-strewn cut beside the tracks for another mile to a meadow. Edith climbed stiffly down from the high hard seat of the big freight wagon and unharnessed her drooping team. She tied them to the wheel spokes and threw them some hay from a bale. Every bone in her body ached from fighting the wagon through mud and swamp, uphill and down and along steep sidehills where the wagon threatened to overturn. She climbed back in, lit a fire in the big stove, put the kettle on, then sat down and sobbed. Her eyes closed of their own accord and she slumped in the chair.

The children's cries woke her; they were hungry. Edith relit the fire and made supper, moving mechanically. She sipped some tea and soup, then followed the children to bed. Fred gnawed jerky and was soon snoring in his own wagon, a blanket over his face against the mosquitoes.

Edith slept uneasily, through nightmares of wagons overturning, swamps, hideous hillsides and rapids. She woke feeling nearly as tired as when she had gone to bed. Hosts of mosquitoes rose from the spongy, rank meadow where they had camped.

She lit the stove and closed the damper for a moment to smoke the mosquitoes out, then untied the tent flap and peered out. The wagon was caked with mud. The horses were almost unrecognizable, matted with clay and grey with the bloodthirsty pests wherever the mud did not cover. Edith looked across the meadow, then sat down hard on the wagon seat and started to laugh, hysterically. Fred, bleary-eyed, looked out from his wagon in alarm.

"What? What is it? What's happened?"

Edith kicked her feet against the splashboard and pointed, voiceless, tears streaming from her eyes, until her voice returned.

"A road! That's what it is, a road! Oh, Fred, look at that, a road right on the other side of the tracks and we drove miles along the right of way when we could have had a dry flat road!"

Wolf Creek

They moved on as soon as the teams could be hitched up, heading for the railhead at Wolf Creek, several miles further west. For the first time in weeks, Edith could drop the reins and let the team pick its way along the tote road.

The road ran through fertile, undulating country, then through dense second-growth timber, never far from the Grand Trunk steel.

The wagons passed by Chip Lake, a small body of water surrounded by thick woods, then wound up a broken, well-wooded country, the hollows bridged by beaver dams. By noon they reached a heavily wooded hilltop and gained their first sight of the foothills of the Rocky Mountains.

The road descended, passing through swamps and in several places the Fryes crossed them on ancient beaver dams as sound as dikes. Indian pears and moose berries grew along the road. Early nightfall found them approaching a cluster of log houses, barns, shacks and one larger building which was a store, restaurant and bar. Fred headed directly for the bar; Edith and the children went into the rude dining area.

A tall, handsome man with black hair and snapping black eyes greeted them.

"You must be Mrs. Frye, am I right?"

"Yes, yes I am," Edith replied, somewhat taken aback.

"I'm Dave Henry," the man introduced himself, "and Fred and I have been on many a trail together."

Cook, sometime guide, and bartender, Henry was a jack of all trades. In Edmonton he had performed with Fred in amateur theatricals at the Elks Lodge; one such play had been commemorated by postcard photographs of Fred and Everett Bogardus in woolly chaps, holding up Henry, playing a bartender. However congenial, though, Henry was indolent and lacked Fred's drive. He was a follower, never a leader.

His thirst slaked, Fred joined the family for dinner and talked the situation over with Dave Henry. Ahead lay Moose Lake, the headwaters of the Fraser River. Only a rough track led around the lake, rocky and narrow, clinging to cliffs which dropped straight down to the water.

Fred proposed to drive the cattle and wagon teams around the lake, and float the wagons down the twelve-mile reach on rafts. However, there was little point in going further west at that stage; construction was lagging behind, and Edith did not want to be stranded in the wilderness with a new baby. Fred decided they would winter at Wolf Creek. He and a crew of men would go on ahead to build the rafts, and he would resume freighting from Edmonton. Daily trains shuttled between Wolf Creek and Edmonton.

After seeing Edith and the children set up comfortably in a small meadow near Wolf Creek, with Dave Henry to help look after the stock, Fred and Roy Loucks boarded the train for Edmonton. Fred was owed a considerable sum for freighting.

The moment he could, Charles, an enthusiastic fisherman, headed for the nearest creek. He returned in late afternoon with a stringer of fish. That night the boy only picked at his food. His forehead was hot and dry to the touch. Edith put him to bed early. Charles spent a fitful night, frequently waking and crying. By morning he was too weak to stand, and his quilt was wringing wet. He did not improve throughout the day and complained that his legs ached. He could not keep food down and threw up when Edith gave him water. Desperate, Edith wrapped him in a blanket and took the next train for Edmonton, covering his eyes against the light which would make him cry.

Edmonton's broad Jasper Avenue was lined with power poles and streetlights. Board sidewalks fronted the stores and crossed the streets at intersections, half buried in the mud. Automobiles were parked in front of some of the buildings. Nearly half the businesses were real estate agencies.

She found the hospital and carried Charles in. The doctor stripped him, asking whether he had been in the bush much.

"He is a dedicated fisherman," Edith said.

The doctor felt through Charles' hair until he encountered a hard lump. He clipped the hair so they could see the half-buried body of the woodtick embedded in his scalp. Cleansing the area, he touched the insect with a hot matchstick and drew out the blood-engorged creature.

"He has Mountain Fever," the doctor explained. "It is caused by woodticks, and removing the tick alleviates the symptoms. It is sometimes fatal, but I think we've caught it in time. Those who recover are immune from the disease; they never catch it again."

Immensely relieved, Edith set off to find Fred. She had to get back to Wolf Creek, and she needed money to pay the hospital bill. At the Grand Trunk office she found that the payroll had not yet come in; Fred was waiting for his money at a nearby hotel. Edith also found that her reputation as the woman who had driven a freight wagon from Olds to Wolf Creek had preceded her. Once her identity was known, people pointed her out on the street.

She found Fred in the bar of the hotel. Roy Loucks had returned to Wolf Creek, and Fred would be back as soon as he had the money in hand. With someone she knew to look after the situation in Wolf Creek, Edith was less anxious. She returned to the hospital to nurse Charles, sleeping on a cot in his room. In a day he had recovered enough to travel, and they boarded the train west to Wolf Creek.

All was in order when Edith arrived back at Wolf Creek with Charles, except that Fred had not returned. Roy Loucks shrugged his shoulders; Edith's heart sank. She knew where he was.

Two days later, Fred staggered off the train at Wolf Creek, roaring drunk. Edith heard the bang of his revolver as he weaved up the hill toward the wagons, howling and bellowing at the top of his lungs. Edith rushed down the hill to meet him, holding her skirts off the ground.

"You're drunk!" she hissed. "Just look at you! Give me that pistol!"

She grabbed at the revolver held loosely in his hand. Fred looked at her dumfounded, then snatched the gun back. He slapped her, knocking her to the ground.

"Neither you nor anybody else tells me what I can and can't do," he snarled, then stamped off.

The children watched, horrified. When Fred was gone Edith rose and stumbled to her wagon. Her ears rang; her face had begun to swell, and she felt as if she had been clubbed. She washed her face and dabbed the blood from her mouth. Edith forced herself to be calm and climbed down from the wagon, to find Fred. He was sprawled beneath a tree, a whisky bottle beside him.

"What do you plan to do, Fred?" she asked flatly. "How long are we going to stay here?"

Fred glanced up and seeing her bruises, looked away.

"I...I'm sorry. I don't know what came over me. I deserve the whip."

Fred followed Edith back to the wagon and drank some coffee, then went to his wagon to sleep it off. In the morning he was up early, fed the stock and made coffee before Edith awoke. There was no need to move on that season, he had decided. With a crew of men he would go on ahead and build the rafts, then head on over the

Yellowhead Pass to Tete Jaune and build a road down to the homestead. If they waited until the next year, the railroad would do a good deal of roadbuilding ahead of them. Because he would be gone for several months, he would hire Dave Henry to look after the stock and do the chores. Henry would also have a good cabin built for Edith.

The men loaded packhorses with axes and adzes, augers, coils of rope and long bridge spikes. They took the grader, scraper and plows, but not much food; they could buy groceries from the railroad camps on ahead.

Edith watched them go, feeling empty. Her relationship with Fred was changing from wife-husband to partners; she needed him, but she had no feelings about him, neither love nor hate.

Summer opened and Edith planted a large garden. The children weeded, and the plot began to show promise. Charles was an independent eight-year-old, and serious little Myrtle bossed Frances and Ella and changed Lottie's diapers. With Dave Henry looking after the cattle, Edith found time to explore the surrounding country. She always took her .45-90 with her, and more than once shot an unwary doe near the cabins.

Railroad construction resumed and life was never dull with the construction to watch. The blasting went ahead. Rock outcroppings were shattered and boulders too large to move by lever or team were blown to rubble. The blasts shook the hills and sent flocks of birds wheeling.

Behind the powder crews came the swampers, hewing timber and slashing brush. They dragged the debris to one side of the right of way, piling tree trunks for the tie makers. Then came teamsters with mules and horses drawing scrapers and fresnoes, wide blades made of hard tool steel, one to a team. The scrapers were tilted by the teamster so their sharp lips bit into the soil like great shovels, then tilted back and dragged to wherever fill was needed. The teamster would trip a release, spilling the dirt in a mound, and return for another load.

Most of the laborers were Chinese and blacks, strong men proud of how hard they could work. Many of the blacks sang as they worked, picking at the ground with grubhoes and shovels. Each had a quota to fill, and the foremen saw that each moved his allotted yardage. There were as many as five hundred men employed at the peak of construction.

They were bossed by a wiry little man named Fred Griffin, an old hand at railroad construction. He kept the men on the bounce and they seemed to work well under him. The work proceeded at the rate of a mile a day when no major obstacles were encountered. When progress was delayed by a difficult stretch of blasting, the right of way crews went on ahead, and returned when the blasting was accomplished.

A second crew of several hundred men a few miles behind leveled the roadbed with horses and mules. A locomotive pulling flatcars loaded with ties and rail followed. The men laid the ties down and then positioned the rail, which was cantilevered out by a sturdy crane on a flatcar pushed ahead of the locomotive.

In the fall, when the cold winds came, Fred returned. Dave Henry had proved to be a good man with the stock, so Fred hired him on for the winter. Henry had put on weight with Edith's cooking, and it was not difficult to persuade him to stay.

The men built a meathouse and spent several weeks hunting. They dug the big crop of potatoes that Edith and Helen Loucks had planted, and the children picked berries to preserve. Trees were skidded in, bucked, split and stacked for firewood, and the houses were banked with earth. Fred unlimbered the mower and cut wild hay from meadows for the horses. The cattle were moved to sheltered winter pasture where they could find plenty of forage beneath the snow.

When the construction halted with the first heavy snows, most of the navvies disappeared. A few built cabins and prepared to spend the winter at Wolf Creek.

In February, Fred developed itchy feet. He went on a trapping expedition, trailing a packhorse. Edith dreaded the long dark winter months cooped up with the children, and faced with the inevitable settling down to a humdrum existence of cooking and child-rearing.

When the warm chinooks blasted down from the mountains in mid-March, she began looking for Fred's return. By then she knew she was pregnant again.

Yellowhead Pass

April was only weeks away when a tramp with inch-long whiskers and clothing greasy-black from wood-smoke and dirt walked into Wolf Creek, leading a horse laden with furs. His eyes glowed from a face burned nearly black from the snow glare. It was Fred. A month of clean living and no whisky had wrought a change in Fred, and Edith welcomed him back.

He luxuriated in clean clothing, a haircut and homecooking for the next weeks until the thaw came in earnest. When the ice and snow had gone from the creeks and the spring sun had begun to banish the last of winter, the men brought the cattle in from the range. Dave Henry and a gang of drovers left a week before the wagons, trailing packhorses, as no wagon could follow the track around Moose Lake. The final drive to British Columbia had begun.

Fred greased the wagons, loaded Edith's precious stove, bolted it in place and stowed the trunks and crates. The children tumbled in, and the baby was tucked into the cradle behind Edith's seat. Edith slapped the reins and the horses, fat after the winter layoff, leaned into the traces.

The road out of Wolf Creek was rutted and rough, as bad as any they had traveled. Wolf Creek crossed the road about half a mile west of the settlement. The cattle's tracks left imprints in the mud at the ford. They crossed creeks several times on the first day. The banks were often steep, and hard on the horses. Occasionally they passed tall spruces shorn of all the branches in the middle of the crown.

Fred explained. "They're lobsticks, sort of a monument. The Indians cut off all the middle branches of a good tall tree and mark your sign at the bottom. You're supposed to live as long as the tree then. You're supposed to give the Indian a handsome present in return."

The second day they passed the Canadian Northern railhead and came into Edson, where the Grand Trunk steel had finished the season. Only the Grand Trunk right of way, and the wagon road that paralleled it, extended west of Edson. The town was a ramshackle affair, but there was a well-stocked general store where Edith bought bolts of cloth for clothing and other necessary supplies. Edith was the first white woman in the territory, and when she introduced herself as Mrs. Fred Frye, the storekeeper stared at her.

"Well, I'll be. I thought Fred was peddling me a line when he said he was a family man. I never believed him. He'd go by, saying the next time he'd come through with you and the family."

The old tote road out of Edson was meant to be a winter road. There were many swamps where the wheel ruts filled with water. The country grew more rugged as they crept closer to the Rocky Mountains. Deep gullies, ravines, bogs and hills slowed their progress. Two days after Edson they came into Obed, where a few Indian tents were spotted beside a small lake. The wagons stopped on a small peninsula for the night. A trout jumped just offshore and Charles was out of the wagon in a flash.

"Look!" he shrilled. "They're jumping!"

Fred grinned and went to his wagon. He pulled out a long leather cylinder with caps buckled on either end.

Unbuckling the container, he slid out a long, slim cloth case, then shook out several slender rods. It was a bamboo flyrod, one of the first ever seen in the territory. He jointed the sections, attached a reel filled with heavy silk line and threaded the line through the guides. He unrolled a long gut leader from an aluminum box and tied it to the line, then tied on a gaudy fly.

"No worm," he explained.

Wading out into the water, he stripped out several yards of line, worked the line out over the lake and gently dropped the fly on the surface. A dimple appeared and the fly vanished as a trout sucked it in. Fred struck and the long rod bent nearly double. The reel shrieked, and Fred worked his thumb into the reel to slow the spinning drum. The line slanted through the water, lifting out close to the rod, and the rainbow jumped, dancing along the surface.

It was a new way of fishing and everyone old enough to hold a rod wanted to try their luck. Fred cut long limber branches and tied on flies for everyone. The shoreline was soon frothing with bright trout.

It was almost dark before they quit, exhilarated with the new sport. For Charles, it was the beginning of an avocation that would last the rest of his life.

As they came away from the lake, a number of Indian women approached and introduced themselves with signs. They gladly accepted some of the trout. In the evening, the little Fryes played with the Indian children until late. The next day, several of the Indian men rode with them, helping bridge the gullies and push the wagons when they bogged down.

The road turned southwest, and two weeks later the wagons caught up with the cattle herd in the low bottom lands of the Athabasca River. Successive terraces, levels of the old river bed, now covered with spruce and pine, stood like steps up to the line of silver-tipped peaks closing the western horizon: the Rocky Mountains, towering sharp and clear. Dusk fell a full hour earlier than on the plains. There was only scanty browse beneath the trees, so the wagons descended to the valley bottom, where they could hear the cattle bawling.

Dave Henry and his crew had run into quicksand at the river bottom, and there was no suitable ford for the wagons. They would have to travel upriver and find another crossing; the far side was higher and drier.

A week later, much of the delay due to the difficulty of herding the cattle out of the swamps, they found a long low gravel bar where the water did not appear too deep, with low banks. Fred and Dave Henry drove the cattle across, with Edith watching from shore. The cattle got to the gravel bar easily, but on the other side the water reached their withers. Fred, leading the herd on his tall mare, dared not turn; the swimming cattle would climb right over him. At last he slid off, and clung to the mare's tail, urging her on. The deep stretch was not long, but to the watchers on shore, it seemed never to end.

Fred looked back to see Edith drive her team into the water. He bellowed to wait, but with the rumble of the wheels on the gravel she did not hear him. They made the gravel bar and plunged into the deep channel on the far side.

With the horses swimming, Edith heard Fred's frantic shouts for the first time. The heavy wagon swung down river. Fred spurred out into the shallows and dropped his rope over the hames of the leading horses. Dave Henry spurred up beside him and did the same. Together, they began to pull the wagon through. Edith's team struck sound footing and hauled the wagon onto dry land. The children were crying; Edith was white-faced, remembering the spectre of the widower who had died in the river in North Dakota.

They double-teamed the other wagons across, and finished the crossing without further incident.

All the way along the Athabasca they lived like kings. They traveled and camped on the high benches, descending in the evening to fish for the big Dolly Varden and rainbow trout, and feasting on the wild fruit that grew along the shore: bland, raspberry-like salmonberries and tart huckleberries.

The trail ran along a terraced alluvial flat nearly free of fallen timber, high above the muskeg. Below, the river wound in and out through treacherous swamps and quicksands. Above stood the mountains, seemingly just over their heads, visible through each small patch of open wood or tongue of prairie. The peaks rose bold and abrupt, five and six thousand feet above the wooded western verge of the prairie at their feet.

At times they could see the survey line of the Grand Trunk Railway on the opposite shore. The task of making a roadbed through that bog was staggering, and Edith wondered if they would ever complete it.

The north-flowing Athabasca grew smaller as they traveled south. They crossed the river again near Jasper House, this time without difficulty. The water barely came up to the axles, and the bottom was sound gravel.

They came back onto the right of way surveyed by the Grand Trunk just past Jasper House. The road opened onto a lakelet surrounded by a semi-circle of mountains: a high wooded hill and Roche à Perdrix on the left, Roche à Myette beyond, Roche Ronde in front and a mountain above Lac Brule, on the left. For half a mile down from their summits, no tree, plant or shrub shaded the stupendous stone that the trappers of old had thought fit to name. The first three peaks were divided by the lake beyond the thick fringe of rushes.

As they traveled on, the country opened, and the colors of Roche à Perdrix were revealed on the lower and inner side. Even the cattle now seemed docile and subdued, impressed by the grandeur. The limestone of Roche Ronde, laid down a million years ago as distinct as the pages of a half-open book, were contorted and twisted by the ancient writhings of the earth.

A wooded hill forced them nearer to the river and around the base of Roche à Myette, now in full view. Its grand bare forehead, nine thousand feet above the sea, filled the background and closed the mouth of the valley.

Fittsue, later called Jasper, was an impressive town, and the Fryes camped beside the lake. The Athabasca River swept away south to take on the name Whirlpool River. That was the road to the Columbia country, over a rugged pass six thousand feet high. The Fryes would go west, along the Myette, into the start of the big timber.

The wagons bumped along a rough road, the

remains of an old pack trail recently widened. Windfalls frequently blocked the way. Often they were firehardened snags which even sharp axes could only dent. Then, Fred would unsling the heavy Gilchrist jack on its carrying strap and jack the log up so it would not bind the saw.

The Myette rushed down a narrow valley, fed at every turn by foaming falls from the hillsides. At some fords, Fred or one of the other men had to wade into the strong current and lever boulders aside so the wagons could cross. In the afternoons, when the hot sun had melted the snowpack, the streams rose as much as a foot, delaying the wagons. They had now entered the Yellowhead Pass.

The Clydesdales stumbled and floundered through foul-smelling marsh mud. Hordes of blackflies assaulted the animals and humans. Edith wound her shawl around her head and the children sweltered beneath blankets, to little avail. The bloodthirsty pests left blood welts on every patch of bare skin. The horses were in agony from the flies and dangerous to approach.

The main branch of the Myette turned north, and then a smaller branch, until both disappeared into the hills. They were soon over the Yellowhead Pass, in British Columbia. High above were the headwaters of the Fraser. Ahead lay Cowdung Lake.

Later named Yellowhead Lake, Cowdung Lake was five miles long, a narrow slab of amethyst below the peaks of the Seven Sisters, clear with a pebbly beach. North, the mountains first glimpsed from the Athabasca weeks before, that had been hidden by the woods at their base as they traveled along the Myette, loomed over their heads: riven masses of stratified rock, a giant jagged crosscut saw of granite.

On the far shore was a small cabin, built by a hermit named McNamara. He despised company, hated the railroads which had come to disturb his peace, and never showed himself. They paused for two days while Fred and Dave Henry made a reconnaissance of the road ahead.

The trail proved to be bad beyond Edith's belief. The corduroy Fred's crew had laid across the swamps the year before threatened to sink, and the wagons jolted over the logs. Worse were the sharp rocks hidden beneath the mud that hurt the horses' hooves.

Five days past Yellowhead Lake, they glimpsed the blue water of Moose Lake through the trees, and a cheer went up. Edith, now heavily pregnant, climbed down and let the lake breeze blow over her. She felt as weary as she ever had, and prayed for the ordeal to end.

Moose Lake

The rafts were moored to shore. They were rigid platforms of logs about thirty feet long and half again as wide, constructed with the Hudson Bay locknotch. The locknotch was two parallel crosslogs, one above, one below, and at right angles to the longer logs. Their protruding ends were lashed together, clamping the long logs. Each raft could support a heavy wagon. There were six of the barges, which lashed together formed two long rafts.

It was a relief to pause after the grueling wagon trip. The women and children fished off the rafts while the men loaded the wagons and lashed them down. They pitched an awning on one raft for the women, and mounted thick tree forks for the long steering oars.

Edith, Helen Loucks and the children would go on one raft, while Fred and Roy Loucks took the other, more heavily laden craft. When all was ready, the men heaved on long poles and thrust the women's raft off. It slowly moved into the current meandering through the ten-mile long lake. Fred and Roy cast off their own mooring lines and poled themselves into the current.

Away from shore the mosquitoes disappeared and a cool breeze feathered the lake. They could talk between the rafts without raising their voices; sound carried a long way across the placid water. The rafts floated within easy earshot of each other the first day.

It was a holiday for all. Charles fished, and everyone cooled their feet in the lake. The effortless drifting after the jolting labor of driving the wagons was almost too good to believe.

By the second day, the women's less heavily laden raft began to move ahead. The men dwindled to a speck far behind them. Late that day a lumber scow propelled by a gasoline engine pushed down the lake and turned toward them. A rowboat trailed behind on a line.

The engine stopped as the scow approached, and a man called out, "Is there a doctor anywhere around?"

"What is the matter?" Edith called back.

"...convulsions," the man replied, indistinctly. He had a Scottish accent.

Edith waved at the man to come over. He climbed into the rowboat and began rowing toward the raft. Edith got her black medicine bag from the wagon, and waited until the man pulled alongside. His companion had had a fit, he explained, and was unconscious.

They found the stricken man outstretched on the deck, as if crucified. His teeth were clenched tight and his eyes were rolled back. He was rigid, his muscles like wood. Edith poured a dram of brandy and trickled it past his teeth. The man swallowed and coughed, then softened into slumber.

"He'll be all right now," the Scot said. "He never remembers anything when this happens."

Thanking her, he rowed Edith back to the raft and quickly returned to the scow. The engine started again, and the scow made a slow turn and headed back up the lake.

Edith and Helen could no longer make out Fred and Roy's raft, and began to worry. If they got into a fast current they could be in trouble. They had not thought to bring an anchor. In the morning, Edith awoke with the solution: her big plow.

Edith and Fred with their first child, Myrtle, *c.* **1901.** Photo by E.O. Holler, Willow City, N. Dakota

Mile 49, also known as Henningville, was a railroad town about a mile west of what is now Tete Jaune Cache. The Canadian Northern Railway turned south toward Kamloops at Mile 49, while the Grand Trunk continued west toward Prince Rupert.

Foley scow loaded with supplies on the treacherous waters of the upper Fraser Canyon, *c.* 1912. Fred Frye, the first man to bring cattle by river to McBride, used a barge similar to this one. Photo by Captain A.B. Hargrave—Mike Frye collection

The B.C. Express unloads freight at Mile 49, *c.* 1913. Many goods were brought up the Fraser River by sternwheeler to supply the railroads. Photo by W. Jowett—Courtesy of Valemount Historic Society

Fred Frye had secured a lucrative contract to supply railroad ties and bridge timbers to the CNR. Here he is marking trees to be cut. Winter was the tie-making season, as the sap was out of the wood (making it easier to cut) and trees could then be skidded to the right of way easily over the snow-covered ground.

Rolette County, North Dakota, *c.* 1906, just before the Fryes left the United States for Canada. Fred Frye is riding in at far right; Myrtle is seated on horse; Frances is wrapped in a blanket and held by a cousin; Charles is the small boy at center; and Edith is in a dark dress, holding a small dog. Her father, Julius Abraham Bronson, is standing at far left.

The Albreda homestead and the tote road Fred Frye built south from Mile 49, where the road crosses Camp Creek.

Thompson Crossing, a rough town about fifteen miles south of the Frye homestead at Albreda. Fred would haul freight from Mile 49 to Thompson Crossing, stopping at the homestead each way to feed and rest the horse teams.

son Crossing Nov. 8 1913

Fred Frye was an enthusiastic amateur actor. He is shown here with Dave Henry, center, and Everett Bogardus, right.

Fred Frye, left, Dave Henry, center, and Everett Bogardus, right—hamming it up for the cameraman in an amateur theatrical, *c.* 1915.

To celebrate the birth of their first grandchild in 1920, Edith and Fred arranged to have this family photo taken in Kamloops.

Front row, left to right: Frances, Mike, Edith, Fred Jr., Fred, Lottie, Myrtle with son Johnnie (Hastings); back row: Ella, Jule, Charles.

Mr. Justice Murphy of the
B.C. Supreme Court
presided over Edith Frye's
court case.

Mike Frye hauled food to a nearby Japanese internment camp during the
Second World War, using this same Red River cart that his father had used
to haul a still to Albreda from Edmonton.

Edith Frye in her later years—shown here with Jule, left, Fred Jr., center right, Lottie, and Mike, right.

Mike Frye, 1979, with the hay rake that his parents brought out from North Dakota in 1906.

An old Imperial Oil barrel, cut out to make a firebox of the type used in making a still, found on the old Frye homestead.

The CN mainline at
Albreda Station—
between Tete Jaune
Cache and Kamloops.

A jumble of moss-covered timbers found in a narrow ravine behind the old homestead. Could this have been the building where Fred Frye concocted his hellish brew?

Edith Frye's headstone, surrounded by wildflowers, lies near her husband's unmarked grave in the family cemetery above Highway 5, which now bisects the homestead.

Dropping the tailgate, Edith and Helen pushed the plow out with their feet and dragged it to the edge of the raft. They knotted a thick rope to the plow and made the other end fast to one of the main raft timbers. Heaving and grunting, they tipped the blade over the edge and half turned it until one handle thrust out over the water. The plow toppled over with a final push, gouging a deep slash in a log. The rope whipped dangerously, then became taut. The raft shuddered and swung to a halt.

Fred and Roy soon came into view. They threw their weight against the steering oars and turned toward the stationary raft. The rafts ground together, and the squeaks of the timbers echoed off the rocky bluffs. They made the rafts fast and crossed over.

"What happened?" Fred demanded. "How did you stop?"

Edith pointed to the taut Manilla quivering from the log. The rafts trembled with the thrust of the current.

"We got lonesome," she explained. "Here we are, ladies of leisure, and no men aboard. So we tied a rope to my big new plow and dropped it overboard. How you're going to get it up again, I don't know for the life of me!"

The men gaped at her. "The plow! That thing must weigh three hundred pounds! How did you ever get it over?"

"Brains and brawn," Helen Loucks said. "Her brains, my brawn."

Edith kindled a fire in her cookstove and made tea while Fred and Roy scratched their heads and stared at the anchor rope. They got down on their knees, then their stomachs, trying to draw up a bight. Arms aching, bellies wet from the waves splashing up between the logs, they were unable to budge it. Finally, they levered the rope up using the long sweep as a lever and broke the plow loose. They easily raised it, hauling hand over hand, and dragged the plow over the edge of the raft, dripping wet but undamaged. From then on, the rafts stayed together.

Their speed increased as the current quickened toward the west end of the lake. The valley began to close in and rock faces glared through the trees. The trail, a barely perceptible ribbon through the trees, crept close to the precipice.

The whine of an engine-driven saw sounded across the lake as the rafts drifted toward the outlet. A substantial wharf on pilings had been built out into the lake. The sound of the saw stopped and a short man came out of the sawmill on the shore. He waved the rafts away from the wharf.

"Too many people! What're those pilgrims doing here? Get off! No landing here!"

The Scottish man who had requested Edith's help on the scow came onto the dock. "You let those people land here!"

The short man turned and stalked back into the sawmill. The other waved them toward the raft, then followed him back into the mill. The sound of the engine resumed.

Fred and Roy heaved on the sweepers and the rafts grated against the pilings, then drifted sideways toward shore. Dave Henry appeared and helped rope the rafts in. They could go no further; ahead, the Fraser River plunged through a deep and narrow canyon. There were places where a person could jump from one side of the canyon to the other, fifty feet above the swirling water.

They were no sooner ashore than the children were running down the gravelly beach to the sawmill, lured by the exotic machinery. The logs were lifted, dripping, from the lake on a chain ramp and drawn into the maw of the mill. They emerged on a deck to be pinned onto a carriage which hurled the logs against a spinning circular saw. Turpentine-smelling cascades of sawdust flowed down an orange volcano beneath the platform. A great drift of sawdust spread under the wharf and over the lake. There were fishlines tied to the wharf, sets for the trout which hid beneath the cloud of sawdust on the surface. Edith literally had to drag the children back to the wagons to eat.

Dave Henry brought up the teams and they drove the wagons off the rafts to a camp in the shade of a spruce grove. They would camp there until they had taken the rafts apart to recover the spikes and rope. The mill would buy the logs.

Edith awoke early the next morning, feeling rested and refreshed. The voyage across the lake had been the best part of the trek. The camp was still asleep when she climbed down from her wagon and walked past the men's tents to the lakeshore. The morning sun slanted across the lake and gilded the drift of sawdust. The brush crackled close to shore.

'One of the horses,' Edith thought.

Then she saw the great shape, too tall for a horse, with a great hump on its back. A moose, black except for a white rump, stood stock still, watching her.

Edith turned back and walked slowly, casually, back to her wagon. She stepped up onto the hub and pulled her rifle from beneath the wagon seat, balancing awkwardly. Levering a cartridge into the chamber, she strolled back to the lake. She moved quietly through the foliage to the fringe of low spruce and willow where the moose had appeared. Ducking beneath a windfall, she moved a fern aside with the rifle barrel and peered up.

The moose stared at her from the far edge of a small clearing. It had the biggest spread of horns Edith had ever seen. They were covered with velvet, tattered at the tines.

Edith lifted the long rifle until the front sight was on the animal's thick neck and settled the bead into the rear sight notch. The rifle bucked as she pressed the trigger and the moose staggered. It wheeled and pounded through the brush toward the camp, spraying blood.

The boom of the rifle rolled and echoed across the lake. Fred sat up abruptly in his tent. He scrambled from his blankets and fell through the opening, directly into the path of the wounded moose. Fred threw himself aside, tripping on the guylines of Dave Henry's puptent, tearing the stakes out and collapsing the canvas.

The moose veered from this terror, and Dave Henry erupted from the wreckage, cursing and looking savage. He fell flat in front of the moose, now standing with lowered head, bloody froth bubbling from its nostrils. Henry jackknifed into a crouch, rose quickly and bolted for the lake. Head up, elbows pumping, long johns flapping in his wake, he tore past Edith. There came a splash as he hit the lake.

Frantically, Fred kicked the guylines loose and dove beneath Edith's wagon. The moose took another step forward, and folded gently onto its side. Edith, tracking the moose with the rifle, lowered the muzzle and let down the hammer. She slid to the ground, her back against a tree and laughed until tears came. Henry waded out of the lake, buttoning himself back together and stalked past her to the moose, approaching it warily. Fred rose out of the ferns beneath the wagon and snorted through his nose at the big man with his great black beard, in grey long underwear.

"What're you gawking at?" Henry snarled. He burrowed into the ruins of his tent to salvage his pants and his dignity.

Roy Loucks appeared with a butcher knife to cut the moose's throat. Helen peered out of her wagon and the children's heads began to pop out of the wagon flaps. Edith sat up, sides aching, rolled onto her knees and stood, holding the rifle.

"So you're the one who caused all this trouble," Henry accused, when he emerged.

Edith nodded her guilt. "I got a chance to shoot a moose, and figured I'd never have a better one, but I didn't know it would do that. You looked so funny..." She began giggling again.

"Well, next time, try to shoot it a little further away from the wagons," Fred said.

It was a while before Fred and Dave Henry could appreciate the hilarity of the situation, but in the end Edith was forgiven. They thrust a stout singletree through the gambrels of the moose and hoisted it to a high branch. When they headed west again, they left the antlers nailed to a tree. Moose Lake had lived up to its name.

The Homestead

———————⟨∞∞∞◎○◎∞∞∞⟩———————

Edith was now nearly full term, and managing the big wagon was almost too much for her. The rough road wound between enormous trees four and five feet thick. The roof of the forest was a hundred feet above their heads. The women, especially, felt dwarfed and oppressed by the size of the trees and the gloom; the scale reduced them to the stature of insects, crawling along the vast, dank forest floor. Fred promised that the enormous spruce and firs would look like matchsticks, compared to the big cedar country ahead.

The little wagon train followed the trail of the cattle herd along the gorge of the Fraser River, the thunder of the water rumbling from the chasm. The air became fresher and crisper, and the insects ceased plaguing. The vegetation of the Pacific slope began to show distinctly. Lighter green cypress mingled with dark woods until it predominated. White birch and small maples appeared. The leaves were beginning to flare into autumn tones high on the mountainside. Numerous streams rushing down to feed the Fraser River blocked their way. Some of the torrents had been rudely bridged by the Grand Trunk surveyors.

It was near evening when they rounded a bend and came out onto a level meadow extending well back toward the mountains. A huge high crag to the north rose to the clouds, its craggy peaks hidden in mist. They all climbed out to stare, awestruck. As they watched, a wind came out of the west. Slowly, the cloud blanket wrapping Robson's Mountain shredded and the stupendous cone of the mountain emerged, towering above the meadow at its base.

Mile Fortynine, also called Henningville, was only another day's journey away. There the Canadian Northern rail would turn south to follow the North Thompson down to Kamloops, while the Grand Trunk continued west toward Prince Rupert.

The valley opened out past Mount Robson. The Fraser River murmured along at a steady flow, zigzagging back and forth across the valley. In the afternoon, the wagons emerged from the timber into a clearing on the Fraser River. Smoke from tents and shanties on the far bank drifted through the trees.

A barge slung on a cable across the river pulled on its moorings on the near shore. Edith drove her wagon down the shallow incline and onto the ferry. There was no one in sight until Fred stood up in his wagon box and bellowed. In a moment a man appeared from the riverbank where he had been dozing, rubbing his eyes. He stared at Edith, sitting straight on her wagonseat.

" 'Pon my word, am I sober or is that a woman on my barge?"

"That there is my missus," Fred growled, "so get her on over."

The ferryman recognized Fred and stepped back, then grinned and slid a bottle out of his coat pocket.

"Well, if it ain't Fred Frye again! What is this here country coming to, women and kids!"

He and Fred shared a drink, then the ferryman hurried down to the slip. The big gasoline motor mounted amidships caught at a pull and Fred cast off the lines. The current thrusting against the barge bowed the thick cable. Foam pushed out at the bow and spray broke over the sides. Edith drove her wagon off at the far end and the ferry returned for the other wagons.

A few Indians appeared at the landing and stared as the wagons came across. Dogs came up from the Shuswap camp on the riverbank and nipped at the horses' legs until some Indian children drove them away with stones.

Henningville was a ramshackle line of log huts, rough plank shanties with canvas roofs and tents, fronting on the right-of-way. Refuse and garbage lay everywhere; the gullies were littered with empty whisky bottles. Here and there a drunk slumbered in the muck.

They drove through the shantytown to a meadow on the Fraser River where Dave Henry had stopped with the cattle. Edith set the wagon brake and wearily climbed over the seat into the wagon to lie down. She closed her eyes and listened to the sound of the camp.

Several horsemen came pounding in, hooting and shouting for Fred. Edith heard him protest facetiously, then ride off. She knew he would not be back that night. Edith gathered her strength and made supper for the children.

Fred returned in the morning, red-eyed and sick. He crawled into his wagon, where he remained for the rest of the day. When he appeared for supper he was sober and somewhat chastened. Fred had been smart enough not to attempt gambling with the Indians. Many of the Indian men were addicted gamblers, as adept with a shaved deck as any white man. There were high stakes games, and the unwary could be parted from everything they owned in an evening.

The homestead was forty miles south of Henningville, and there was only a rough track. It would take several weeks to widen and grade the road so the wagons could get through. Fred had planned on bossing the road crews himself, but opportunity beckoned. Pat Burns at McBride was paying a high price for beef for the Grand Trunk Railway. Fred hired a crew to build the road and dispatched them south while he and several other men built five large rafts to float the cattle down to McBride.

The rafts were forty feet long by thirty feet wide, with

good solid sides made of jackpine poles. It took eight men to steer each raft with long poles and sweeps. With the loaded cattle bellowing and roaring, and the cowboys turned boatmen cursing, the rafts pushed out into the current and floated west toward McBride.

All the rafts made it safely, although there were some close calls. At McBride they were poled into the wharf at the mouth of Oil Creek where Burns had built his slaughterhouse. It was the first shipment of cattle by river to McBride.

When Fred returned he went south to oversee the roadbuilding. With the men gone, the women settled into a lazy routine, basking in the late August sun. Edith scrubbed and arranged her wagon, boiled bedclothes and carefully laid them away for when her time came.

The weather grew hotter and more humid as September began, until the women felt they could stand it no longer. Trapped in their long dresses, they suffered more than the men. The nights were sultry and mosquitoes infested the wagons. They stuffed newspapers inside their stockings to keep off the bloodthirsty pests.

The long strain of the trek, her pregnancy and the unrelenting heat left Edith with painful backaches. Her legs were swollen and she felt bloated. She longed to lie down in a cool dark room with a damp cloth over her eyes and just simply rest.

When her labor started in earnest on September 10 she was still exhausted. The delivery was difficult and prolonged, and when the squall of a baby boy broke the air the next day Edith was almost too far gone to care.

Her milk did not flow and there was no cow milk available, and the baby, Mike, failed visibly. He spit out the thin gruel the girls prepared for him and howled. Edith was not growing any stronger either. At last, the heat spell broke, and with the cooler weather Edith's milk flowed. There was great relief in the encampment; baby Mike was the first white child born on the west of the Yellowhead.

When she felt stronger, Edith made a sling and carried the baby papoose-style to the Shuswap village. She was escorted to a tent where she set the sling down and opened it. Mike stared up, not at all displeased to see a circle of dark faces above. The Indian women complimented Edith and exclaimed over the baby's fair skin, although he was not a great deal fairer than many of the native babies.

One Shuswap woman hurried away and returned with her husband, talking and gesticulating toward the baby. That evening, the couple came to Edith's wagon and through gestures offered to trade a handsome horse for Mike. Edith was not offended, and gave the couple coffee.

When Fred returned toward the end of September, Edith presented him with his new son and told him about the offer.

Fred laughed, delighted with the gurgling baby boy.

"Maybe we should of taken them up on it. What kind of horse was it?"

"If it'd been one of the others I would have," Edith sighed, looking at her children racing around the camp with the Shuswap children. "They're so dirty most of the time I can hardly tell them apart from the little Shuswaps."

They forded the river in late September at a place where the currents built a sandbar each year after the freshet, and headed south. Baby Mike rode in an applebox on the wagon seat beside Edith, well-padded against the jolts.

At first the traveling was easy, over smooth sandy soil with little undergrowth along the ridge of a wide hogback. The black pines on the rise grew well apart and there was little difficulty maneuvering the wagons between them. On the third day they came upon the valley of the Canoe River, stretching west. They crossed the Canoe early in the morning before the sun on the glaciers above had time to swell the flood.

From there on the road deteriorated; small swamps and muddy streams slowed their progress. Brittle, spiny Devil's Club grew in nettlesome clumps. Ferns ranging from tiny clusters to great masses six feet high covered the forest floor.

The road twisted along broad gravel benches like

terraces toward the summit of the Camp River, dividing the Thompson and Columbia watersheds. At the top, the trail dropped into a new valley, winding through sandy jackpine forest.

They bumped along a steep sidehill. Edith braced herself with one leg to keep upright. A wheel mounted a boulder and the wagon lurched. The lower wheels dropped into a rut and the load shifted. Edith scrabbled for the applebox as the upper wheels tilted, lifted into the air and the wagon overturned, pitching her out. The sound of splintering wood and the rip as the anvil and forge tore through the canvas filled the air. The horses whinnied in terror as they were pulled down. The applebox tumbled past Edith and rolled downhill, followed by the anvil.

Everything was suddenly silent, except for the horses. Edith scrambled on hands and knees, heart pounding, to the applebox. It was lying right side up at the base of a bush. The baby stared up, unhurt. Edith lifted him out and held him close. The infant, sensing her fright, began to howl.

Bruised and battered, the other children clambered out of the wagon. The men rushed back, horrified.

"Edith! Are you all right? The baby?" Fred bent over her.

"I'm all right. The baby's fine. Oh, Fred, how much farther?" Edith groaned.

Helen Loucks helped Edith to Fred's wagon, where she lay down. She came in with a washrag to clean Edith's scrapes, then tended to the children. No one had been seriously hurt.

The men cut the horses free and righted the wagon with block and tackle. The stove had been torn loose from its bolts and the chimney pipe was crumpled. Soot coated everything inside. Several of the bows were snapped, but otherwise the sturdy wagon was undamaged.

The next day they crossed Starvation Flats, a plantless, rutted sandtrap which threatened to live up to its gruesome name. The wagons sank deep into the sand, and they had to trudge hundreds of foot-dragging yards to cut brush and branches to stuff under the wheels after they had jacked them up.

Days later they reached the homestead. Fred turned the wagons into a clearing where a sizable log cabin stood and climbed down.

Thickly wooded slopes rose on both sides of the valley. The back of a beaver broke the clear calm of a pond across the stream that threaded through the trees. The beaver's tail smacked the water and it dove in alarm.

At the head of the valley was the great mass of Mount Albreda, cradling its glacier in a deep cirque. Edith closed her eyes and listened to the quiet. She remembered her farm at Rolla, the beautiful ranch at Bearberry, and the vision of her rich grazing lands nearly overwhelmed her. She opened her eyes to the thick cedar forest and the clearing. A cold breeze moved down the valley from the great glacier. She climbed down to make her new home.

White Lightning

The front door of the cabin faced south to the Albreda Glacier. There were two big rooms and a woodshed the full width of the house attached to the back. A trap door opened over a roomy cellar dug beneath the back room.

With her cookstove installed in the back and a heater stove in the front room, Edith felt more at home. The log house with its pole and sod roof seemed almost luxurious after the rigors of the trail. The floor was smooth puncheon hand-hewn with adzes.

Fred dug a roothouse deep into the hillside above the cabin and lined and roofed it with cedar logs. He hung a double-thick wooden door on heavy forged hinges to secure their food against animals, and added a massive padlock against any human pilferers. When that was done he hired a crew to put up a barn sixty by eighty feet. He mowed the wild hay and put up fodder for the winter.

Edith was nearly content. The children had taken to the mountain valley, riding and exploring, and Charles fished daily along the stream. She worried about Fred, though. He rose at dawn and drove himself until after dusk, fencing, clearing, cutting wood, tending stock and riding out to locate stands of wood suitable for ties. He seemed distracted and barely noticed Edith or the children. Edith put his odd behavior down to the enormous amount of work he was doing and hoped it would change.

When winter descended Fred began freighting for the Canadian Northern, bringing building supplies and food from Mile Fortynine south to Thompson Crossing, a rough settlement fifteen miles south of the homestead. When he arrived at the homestead he would stop overnight to rest and grain the teams. His schedule worked so he would be home for two nights running, then he would be gone for a week or longer on the long leg forty miles north.

Fred had secured a lucrative contract to supply railroad ties and bridge timbers to the Northern. Cutting rights were available with a minimum of red tape, and while on his freight route Fred had ample opportunity to locate suitable pine stands. The ideal timber was eleven to fifteen inches in diameter, large enough to allow a face eight inches wide to be hewn with a broadax. The tie-making season was from November to April or May, when the sap was out of the wood. The ties were skidded to the right of way when there was snow on the ground.

Fred's odd behavior continued after he started freighting. The squeak of iron-shod runners on the crystalline snow and the jingle of a harness announced his arrival late one long winter night. Clean snow glimmered under the moon. Fred had removed the wheels from the freight wagon and replaced them with runners. The team snorted and stamped in the Arctic cold.

In her warm pallet in the kitchen, Edith heard Fred's footsteps in the snow as he forked hay to the horses. A gust of cold air heralded his entrance. Fred filled his plate and sat down by the stove. Edith drifted back to sleep, expecting him to come to bed after he had finished the supper she had saved for him in the warming bin on the back of the stove.

Hours later, she awoke with a start. The quilts were cold beside her. Fred had not come to bed.

Outside in the brittle cold, Fred had jacked up the big wagon and dismounted one of the runners. The barrels of flour he was carrying were stacked in the snow beside the wagon. He emerged from the blacksmith shop by the barn with the heavy oaken runner, a bright weld showing where one of the iron plates had been annealed.

Fred slid the runner back onto the axle, bolted the hub on, then lowered the sleigh. He tossed the heavy iron jack into the wagonbox and kicked through the snow to the barrels. He rolled one of the four-hundred-pound barrels onto a knee, hefted it with both hands and heaved it into the wagon box. When the barrels were loaded, roped down and covered with a tarp he brought the team up and harnessed it. He was gone before Edith rose.

He returned the next night, making the trip back from Blue River easily with an empty sleigh. Night fell early, and it was dark and cold when he arrived. Edith could hear the team shifting in harness, stamping their feet. Fred filled their nosebags, threw a thick horse blanket over each and went into the blacksmith shop.

A handful of kindling, some bark, a match and a few cranks of the bellows fan, and heat began to well into the log shed from the forge. Fred pulled a whisky bottle from his coat pocket and sat down on a stump by the anvil, staring out the open door, motionless. Time seemed to whirl past. The empty bottle clattered from his hand and he started. The moon had passed through half its arc, and the cabin was dark, only a dim light glowing through the scraped deerhide of the kitchen windows.

He rose, stiff from the cold and his trance and went into the cabin, moving softly. Edith did not stir in her bed; the children were asleep in the front room. Fred sat down by the warm kitchen stove and drowsed, formless thoughts and nightmares of pursuit slipping into his whisky sleep.

When Edith awoke, he was gone again. A puddle by the stove revealed where he had sat, catatonically still, until dawn. The trampled snow and droppings outside showed that the team had stood in its frozen, galling harness the entire night. Edith tried to dismiss her fears but was left with a lingering unease.

When the road turned to impassable gumbo in the spring, Fred threw himself into the labor of clearing his hundred and sixty acres. He and his crew dropped the big cedars with ax and crosscut saw and bucked the trunks into sections so the teams could skid them to a site near the barn where he planned to build a huge bunkhouse for the railroad gangs.

They wrenched out the stumps with the powerful work horses. Sometimes Fred had to jar the larger stumps loose with blasting powder, carefully inserting the fuse, then crimping the stick with his teeth. He worked from sunup to sundown until a large field was cleared. Edith and the children picked rocks and roots, throwing them onto a stoneboat to be hauled to the edge of the field. When it was cleared Fred plowed and seeded hay and prepared a large garden plot near the cabin.

Early in May news of the sinking of the Titanic arrived. Charles M. Hayes, president of the Grand Trunk and Grand Trunk Pacific Railways, was numbered among the "heroic men" who willingly stood back to make room for the women and children in the few lifeboats of the doomed ocean liner. He had set sail for Europe to raise funds for the financially beleaguered railroad, and his death sent shudders through the stock market. Tremors were felt along the right of way through the Yellowhead Pass.

When the roads reopened in early summer Fred departed for Edmonton for the pay he was owed. He made a side trip to Calgary to apply for Canadian citizenship. He was naturalized under the name Fred Charles Frye on July 22, 1912, listing his residence as Bearberry, Alberta, and his occupation as "farmer." Since the law then in force stated that wives and any minor children automatically assumed the man's citizenship, there was no separate listing for them.

Fred returned with a Red River cart groaning under a load of sacks of rye, barley, sugar, crates of glass sealing jars, sheets of copper and coils of copper tubing: the machinery to brew his deadly moonshine. Edith's heart sank but there was little she could do. They lived outside the reach of the law.

Fred built a sturdy cabin in the willows that grew thick around a small spring above the homestead and brought in his materials. After carefully inscribing the shapes on the copper sheets, he cut them out with a cold chisel. The bottom was a large disk. With a wooden mallet he beat the disk into a shallow saucer with an upturned rim. A rectangular sheet of copper fit around the rim to make a cylinder, the edges riveted together. Next, he molded a sloping shoulder and a short neck with a tight cap. In the neck he drilled a hole to insert the worm of copper tubing which would carry off the spiritous exhalation of the still. At the base he cut a hole and soldered in a short pipe to drain the residue.

The worm was a corkscrew of tubing which ran through a water-filled trough made from a cedar trunk. The still was heated by a firebox of clay and stones beneath it. At one side Fred made a shallow groove to funnel the runoff when he drained the still.

When all was ready, Fred filled the still with water and added a mixture of ground rye and barley. He kindled a fire in the firebox and the mash soon began to boil. After an hour of stirring to keep the grain from burning on the bottom, he drained the mash into a barrel. He added more water and sugar to fill the barrel to the top, then poured in a cup of yeast.

After a long day he had four barrels of fermenting beer. Cheesecloth tied across the top of each barrel kept out insects attracted to the sweet nectar.

After a week of fermentation the beer was ready to run. Fred skimmed the thick foam off and siphoned a barrel into the still. He brought it to a boil slowly. A rumble sounded and a gout of steam belched through the hole in the neck. Fred slid the worm into the hole and sealed it with pitch. After several minutes a thin stream of pale liquid erupted from the end of the worm to be caught in a small cask.

When the run was finished, Fred added the second barrel of beer. When that run was completed, he poured the two small casks of distillate back into the still and ran them through a second time, "doubling" the brew and raising the proof considerably. When he tossed a few drops of the double-rectified brew into the coals of the firebox they burst into blue flame. The stuff was proper busthead, he judged, and began filling quart-sized canning jars.

Moonshine, white lightning, dynamite, hooch, it went by many names and looked like clear water, but pure it was not. The unsteady temperature of the fire evaporated not only the alcohol, but the fusel oils which had formed as a byproduct of fermentation. These volatile oil liquids, used in greater concentrations to make lacquer and solvents, could have been removed by filtration through finely ground charcoal or prevented from evaporating by maintaining a lower temperature. However, purity was no concern of the bootlegger. The sole criteria by which his brew was judged was its potency. It could be, and sometimes was, unaffected by filtration through a foot of mud and dung. This occasionally happened when corrupt police officers would pour out a confiscated barrel of moonshine, only to recollect it in barrels buried beneath the sod.

When all the beer was run, Fred started more. He carefully locked the cabin and carried the filled crate of sealers to the cellar beneath the cabin. Henceforth, he would divide his time equally between making moonshine and bossing his tie-making crews. There would be plenty of demand for both products when the railroad construction crews arrived.

The surveyors came in mid-July. Instead of marking the roadbed on the far side of the valley, they pounded a line of stakes right through the Frye homestead.

There could be no change, Fred learned. Canadian Northern Superintendent Hanna had set the maximum allowable grade at half a per cent a mile, no more than twenty-six feet of rise in any mile, taking both grade and curvature into account. Revenues would plummet if more grade was allowed. The Manitoba and North Western, with grades of up to three point one, had been nearly bankrupted because it had to put extra engines on its trains.

The right of way cut a swath through the Frye homestead, alienating much of the land Fred had cleared.

Camp Creek was rerouted, and seepage ruined much of the hay; the young shoots turned black and mildewed. Albreda Lake, which flowed both ways from opposite outlets into the Canoe and Thompson drainages, was drained.

All was not lost, however: the Canadian Northern paid a generous settlement of seven hundred dollars to compensate for the damage. In addition, Fred negotiated a contract to feed and house the construction gangs when they arrived. Fred hired men to build an enormous bunkhouse next to the barn, and brought Dave Henry in to cook. He opened a tie camp at Swift Creek, where the town of Valemount would one day stand. When the clearing crews arrived in the fall, he was ready.

Tie contracting was big business. There was great demand for ties, since an untreated tie would last only about ten years. Tie contractors charged ten cents a tie for their services, on a base rate of sixty to seventy cents a tie. The contractor paid for the roads which snaked along water-courses from the right of way to the tie camps among the pine stands, for the equipment, and the teams to skid the ties out. The contractor paid the Forest Service charges and the loaders' wages.

Makers earned twenty cents a tie and were charged a dollar a day for board. A good maker could produce between twenty and thirty ties a day.

The loaders were the highest-paid laborers in the tie industry, for good reason. Few men could withstand the brutal routine of loading. The loader would pull a tie off a stack with a hooked iron bar, upend the tie, duck beneath it, wrap both arms around the tie and straighten up. Balancing it on one padded shoulder, the loader had to walk up a slanting gangplank onto a flatbed railcar and throw the tie down. Loaders were paid a cent a tie, and could earn from ten to fifteen dollars a day. A few rare women loaded ties.

Fred established several tie camps between Swift Creek, ten miles north of the homestead, and Blue River, fifteen miles south. The older children helped skid the ties out to the right of way, while the younger ones peeled the ties.

Albreda boomed with the start of the construction. Fred's boarding house was jammed with men, and the barn was packed with horses, mules and oxen. He built a blacksmith shop which grew into a machine shop, next to the barn. The front room of the cabin became a roadhouse. Edith hung a heavy canvas curtain over the doorway to the kitchen for privacy, and tried to keep the children away from the bar, where fights frequently broke out. Many tried, but no one bested Fred Frye.

The first locomotive arrived late in the fall. It stopped opposite the roadhouse and a long screeching whistle squealed across the field. Edith and the children ran out to see it; they were passed by the crew, heading for the roadhouse.

An hour later, the train crew weaved back to the locomotive. While the fireman heaved cordwood into the firebox to build up steam, Fred hitched a team to the cow catcher; the grade was too steep for the small engine to gain traction. One of the Clydesdales snorted and reared at the puffing locomotive. Fred hauled the horse down and took the halter between his teeth.

"Watch this!" he grunted through clenched teeth, and fanned the horse with his hat.

The nervous horse reared, picking Fred off the ground, hanging only by his teeth. The tipsy trainmen cheered, awed. It was a feat of strength few could duplicate.

When the horse came down, Fred bound a bandana over its eyes, then led the team ahead. The small locomotive's driving wheels slipped, squealing, then began to pull ahead. The fireman pulled the pin holding the harness to the cow catcher and Fred trotted the team off the track as the machine gathered speed.

The construction crews moved on the next year, but business at the roadhouse continued unabated. Fred's pockets overflowed with money and he spent it freely, on himself, on machinery and equipment, but little on his family.

Edith was constantly tired from nursing, baking, cooking, laundering, making soap, sewing and trying to look after the children, as well as coping with her intractable husband. Her life seemed endless drudgery. She had no time for leisure, no opportunity to groom. Just existing took all her strength, and she felt old and worn before her time.

Terror at Albreda

The advent of World War I the next year brought a
strange tranquility to the valley. Most of the young single
men disappeared, either to the charnel fields overseas or
to peaceful, remote traplines beyond the reach of con-
scription boards. The war generated a local depression,
but the market for moonshine continued unabated, and
the war effort demanded poles for telegraph and tele-
phone lines, pilings and docks.

The last spike was driven in the Canadian Northern
on January 14, 1915, making it a transcontinental
railroad. With the advent of regular, convenient rail
transport to Kamloops, Fred began to disappear for
weeks and months whenever he was flush with money. He
would return penniless and debauched, and would drive
the children to the bush to cut ties.

As the rotgut whisky he consumed fed the black side
of his character, Fred became obsessed with his daughters' budding sexuality. His inhibitions crumbled with the
assault of the moonshine eating at his brain, and his
obsession grew into a compulsion, like a poisonous
fungus spreading in a dark place. The girls learned not to

be alone with him.

Edith knew little of this; the girls were reluctant to say anything, fearing that they would not be believed. Such an episode, committed by a parent whose authority and right may not be denied, represses confession to another. Edith was permanently tired; sometimes she wondered if she would ever awake and not feel weary. What happened during the depths of her exhausted slumber she could not know. As far as she was aware, life was going on in its dreary pattern.

The children excelled at the healthy outdoor labor. The younger ones helped skid ties out to the railroad line and peeled them, while the older children did the heavy work of falling and hewing. Ella and Frances could rival any male tie-makers Fred could hire. One day, when Ella was fifteen and Frances seventeen, competing against one another, they each cut thirty railroad ties. Frances was the steadier worker, but Ella, who alone among the children had inherited Fred's unique physical strength, was capable of extraordinary bursts of exertion. Ella was the loader; she could pack the eight-foot long ties, weighing between two and three hundred pounds, all day long with hardly a pause. On a dare she once carried two number-one ties and a smaller, number-two tie, up a gangplank and onto the flatcar.

Edith was forty-two years old and pregnant in 1915. In February of that year she summoned neighbors to help her deliver the baby. She was deep in labor when a blizzard struck, dumping twelve feet of snow into the valley.

Edith named the boy Jule, after her father. When the weather cleared, the railroad gangs came to dig out the track. Edith snowshoed out with the baby to watch them cut trenches in the snow down to the tracks where the drifts were too deep for the rotary plows. Where the snow had compacted into blue ice, the navvies chopped vertical slots with picks and axes and levered the frozen slabs out like great blocks of marble. The slabs were shattered with sledge hammers into manageable pieces and heaved out.

The imposition of Prohibition in 1917 only served to better Fred's fortunes. A river of moonshine flowed from

Tete Jaune Cache on down through the narrow valley. Fred made frequent trips to Kamloops, where he was by then well known. On one of these excursions he acquired a .45 calibre Colt automatic pistol, Model 1911. He carried it slung in a shoulder holster under his coat.

As his drinking increased, so did his bizarre behavior. If anyone crossed him he would fly into a rage, cuffing and beating Edith and the older children. For some reason, the younger children usually escaped his brutalities. Fred began imagining marauders at night, and took to keeping his shotgun under the bed. When the fit was upon him he would rush out and fire blasts into the night, then sit up with a jar of moonshine until morning. Edith would sit up with him, trying to calm him, and on guard against what he might do next. Fear kept her awake, and the sleepless nights turned her haggard.

Infrequently, Fred would take the family to Kamloops, and while there treated them as generously as he was miserly at the homestead. They usually stayed at the Leland Hotel.

Edith was forty-four years old in 1918 when Fred Jr. was born. She thought he would be her last child, and she was not unrelieved. Myrtle had fled the homestead to marry the son of a McBride rancher, and that was one less pair of hands to help. Edith had wondered about Myrtle's abrupt departure, but the girl had said nothing and Edith was not unhappy to see her leave the nest.

The Grand Trunk Railway was on the verge of bankruptcy that year, a situation brought on in part by the war. Within three years, the Grand Trunk and the Canadian Northern would be amalgamated into the new Canadian National Railway.

In 1919 Edith bore another boy, whom they named Richard. Early that winter, influenza swept down the valley. The epidemic wasted Albreda; everyone was sick. The baby wasted to a skeleton in a week of fever and diarrhea, fouling his wrappings until they all despaired for his life. One morning they found him cold in his swaddling. It was the first baby Edith had lost, and she grieved. Fred scraped the snow from a level patch of ground beside a huge boulder on the hillside above the

103

cabin and hacked a tiny grave in the frozen soil. More than one grave was dug in the valley before the plague eased, then disappeared as suddenly and inexplicably as it had appeared. The only consolation that year was the birth of a son, Jonnie, to Myrtle.

Fred and Edith were delighted with their first grandchild, and made plans to have a family portrait taken in Kamloops. Myrtle caught the Grand Trunk to Tete Jaune Cache and transferred to the Canadian Northern to Albreda. At Kamloops, the train paused on the Indian Reservation across the river, then backed into the city over a temporary bridge over the North Thompson to let the passengers disembark.

Fred left them at the hotel while he went on a mysterious errand. He walked directly to a livery stable where a crank-operated gas pump with a glass measuring bowl on top proclaimed one of the city's first automobile dealerships: J. McCannel & Son, Ford, Overlander, Cadillac. In the showroom stood a gleaming black Chevrolet with yellow spoked wheels and shiny black tires. Fred paid cash for the beautiful machine and ordered several barrels of gasoline to be delivered to the train depot.

Edith took the children shopping for new clothes. She bought Frances and Lottie new dresses, and a jacket and hat for Ella. Mike was fitted out in a wool Norfolk jacket with a belt. Jule received a pair of short pants and a new jacket, and Charles emerged from the store wearing a new jacket.

The photo was taken against a fabric background that included a stained glass window. The photographer posed Fred and Edith side by side on a short loveseat with elaborately carved arms and feet. Fred Jr. sat on Edith's lap and Jule stood on the seat between his parents. Frances sat on a bench angled at Edith's right, holding Mike's hand. Myrtle was seated on a chair at the other side with her baby on her lap. Lottie stood between Myrtle and her father, while Charles and Ella stood behind the love seat. Fred ordered enough prints for everyone, including some to send to relatives.

When they came out of the studio he led them to the

automobile dealership. Edith was aghast, and no one would ride with him in the devilish contraption, so Fred climbed in alone and started the car. He led a grand procession through the city streets to the train depot, the children running behind, shouting, Edith and Myrtle carrying the babies, following more sedately. At the depot Fred managed to stall the car before he hit anything.

There was no question of driving the car back to Albreda; no road existed, so the car was loaded onto a flatcar and chained down. Fred still drove the Chevrolet home, though. He sat behind the wheel of the car the entire distance, sipping from a bottle of whisky and savoring the luxurious feel of the upholstery and the pungent new car smell, a cologne of fresh leather, gas, oil and new rubber.

The arrival of the first automobile created a sensation in Albreda. Eight men helped lift the car down. Most of the children had overcome their fear and boarded for the ride back to the homestead. Not far from home, Fred turned on the rutted track to avoid a boulder protruding from the mud. The outside wheels slipped over the bank and the car teetered. Ella, holding Mike on her lap, tossed him out as the car slid sideways and stopped against a tree. They were bumped and bruised but no one was hurt seriously. Fred brought a team back and pulled the car onto the road.

This time he made it safely to the homestead and drove down the steep bank into the yard. He steered round and round the buildings, bumping over hummocks, through shallow gullies and across the fields until the car ran out of gas and the engine expired. He tromped back to the cabin grinning from ear to ear.

"I don't know when I've had so much fun."

The first warm breezes of the spring of 1922 brought with them the first mosquitoes. The bloodseekers whined unnoticed as Fred, carrying several grain sacks and a big T-handled auger, slipped through the brush to a siding where several grain cars waited. The birds, busy at the scattered grain spilled from the cracks, scattered at his approach. Fred checked for a watchman, then slipped beneath a boxcar loaded with grain destined for the terminals of Vancouver.

He stabbed the worm of the drill into the splintered and blackened bottom of the boxcar and twisted the handles. The bit was keen and sliced easily into the sound wood. Clean yellow shavings crisped out of the hole, and he shifted so they would not fall into his eyes. The drill broke through the wood and he pushed it up, reaming a hole through the thick paper lining the boxcar. A few grains of wheat spiraled out from the threads of the auger. Fred spread a sack beneath the hole, then yanked the drill out. A stream of hard prairie wheat hissed down. When the sack was full, Fred heaved it aside and filled another. When he had filled all the sacks, he stopped the flow of grain with a bung he had whittled earlier, hammering it tight with the heel of his palm.

Alberta had gone dry in July, 1916, and although Prohibition would end in Canada the next year it was difficult to buy large orders of sugar within the province. It was no problem to order sugar from outside Alberta, however, and the regular shipments of grain which went through Albreda made it unnecessary for Fred to buy grain at all.

Fred dragged the sacks from beneath the boxcar, tied them shut and slung them over his back. The beer would brew well during the warm days to come. He walked steadily up the tracks to the homestead, and the still.

When the run was finished, Fred emptied the mash into buckets and carried them back to the cabin. He heaved the cooked and fermented grain onto a bare patch of ground beside the cabin which testified to the lethal qualities of the brew. The chickens ran to the mash, clucking and cackling, then the calf wandered up and nosed the chickens aside. Minutes later the calf staggered off and bumped gently into a tree. It let out a long, quavering moo and folded softly to the ground, neck outstretched. One of the chickens hiccoughed, shook its head to clear its crop and wobbled unsteadily down the bank.

The stockpile of moonshine grew steadily throughout the spring. Fred was drunk for weeks at a stretch, rarely leaving the homestead. Often he would sit catatonically still for hours, never twitching, his jar of whisky untouched beside him until the spell broke.

Fearful of what he might do if left alone, Edith stayed as close to him as possible, and she bore the brunt of his rages. She would try to calm him after his fits and take him to bed, but most often he would sit up with his whisky until morning.

The hellish unpredictability of Fred's rages continued through the summer of 1922 until Edith despaired for the family's safety. She feared for herself and even more so for the children. At last, she took the step she had dreaded for so long.

"Frances," she told the older girl, "go to the depot and have Mr. Arnold send for the police. Tell them to come get your father. Don't let him see you go!"

Frances hurried off, looking nervously for her father, and found the operator. The message was sent off to Red Pass, the nearest provincial police detachment, and Frances returned home, undetected.

A day later two constables arrived. All appeared normal on the homestead when they apprehended Fred, however, and he came with them peacefully to the railway depot.

The constables did not take Fred into custody, however. He was an actor and a good talker, and could put anyone at his ease. While there may have been some substance to the complaint that he had been making whisky, bootlegging was the most common crime on the criminal calendar, and if drinking was technically illegal, it was widely tolerated. And Fred Frye was a well-known tie contractor and a businessman of some substance. He was a charter member of the Kamloops Elks Lodge, formed in 1921, and a popular actor in the charity shows the lodge frequently held. Fred stormed home, stiff-legged with rage.

Frances was in the front room when the door was battered open and Fred exploded in. She saw his knobby fist swinging at her face, then red, then nothing.

"You put her up to this!" Fred screamed at Edith

and knocked her to the floor. He backhanded Ella, sending her reeling, then stalked off to his haunts.

Edith and Ella collected themselves and laid Frances on her pallet. Her face was swollen purple from the blow and she breathed loudly from her mouth. Both her eyes were blackened. The girl did not regain consciousness until the next morning. Edith slept badly, her nose plugged with blood.

"From now on," she told the children, "I want one of you with me always. I am afraid of what your father might do.

"Frances, Ella, go out to the roothouse and make a bed for the little ones. They'll be safe in there. Take plenty of blankets and some candles. I just don't know what else to do."

It was cool and damp inside the heavily timbered root cellar, but not cold. The scent of raw earth and potatoes rose from the floor. Edith and her daughters fashioned a rough crib, padding the splintered wood with sacks. She fed the little children, Fred Jr., Jule, Mike and Lottie, and pushed them into the dank cellar.

"You'll be safe inside here," Edith told them.

She swung the heavy door to and closed the big padlock, hiding the key inside her shirtwaist on a string.

Fred beat her bloody when he discovered what she had done, but he did not break into the root cellar. Over the next several weeks, into the fall, he continued to explode into violence, screaming at the top of his lungs. Edith and the children were virtually prisoners on the homestead, never knowing when Fred might explode into a murderous fit. They were all in total terror of him, and he threatened harm to the children should Edith ever again summon the police.

When the fits came on him, Edith or one of the older children would rush the little children to the root cellar and lock them in. Edith usually bore the brunt of his rages. Bruised and bloody when they were over, she would go out to the root cellar and feel around in the darkness to make sure the children were unharmed.

Only once did they try to summon the police. Charles made a furtive foray for the railway depot. He was halfway there when Fred exploded out of the bush and knocked him to the ground. He kicked the spindly boy all the way back to the cabin and hurled him inside.

The neighbors sensed that something was amiss on the Frye homestead, but they dared not interfere. Fred Frye was not a man to cross, and if his wife did not see fit to complain it was nobody else's business. To the outsider, all seemed normal on the Frye place.

In mid-June that year, an unfamiliar sound droned through the timber. It rose and fell, a gasoline engine laboring. Something gleamed briefly between the trees. Fred came out of the barn and stared as a mud-caked automobile bumped along the rutted road from the north. The car turned down the bank and lurched to the machine shop beside the barn.

Two men climbed out. They were Charles Neimeyer and Frank J. Silverthorne, from Edmonton, bound for Victoria to publicize the need for a highway through the Yellowhead Pass and south to Kamloops. Their Overland automobile was loaded with twelve hundred pounds of equipment, including four twelve-foot planks for crossing washouts and gullies.

The first automobilists through the Yellowhead, they had to build corduroy for literally miles between Edmonton and Jasper. For the most part they followed the old Grand Trunk right of way which had been abandoned when the railway went bankrupt during the war, and great spans of track had been taken up. From Jasper they followed the Canadian Northern line to Henningville, and from there took the tote road south to Albreda. On the last stretch they had broken a spring bracket, and had learned that Fred Frye had a machine shop.

Fred was a competent machinist. He cut loose the broken bracket with a cold chisel and a sledge, then fired up the forge to make a new one. The children crowded around the car, and Mike grabbed the crank of the rotary bellows to fan the fir bark to a high heat.

Fred laid the iron on the glowing bark to heat and soften before he bent it into shape. He lifted the metal out with tongs when it glowed red and laid it on the anvil to bend the flanges. As he hammered, a smoking hot splinter of iron flew off, driving into Mike's bare ankle.

It felt like a pinprick for a moment, and then Mike yelped. A curl of smoke lifted up from his leg and red blood welled out. Edith hurried up and took him away. The bleeding stopped after she bound a flour-filled cloth over it, but the iron splinter remained buried in the boy's leg just above the ankle.

Fred refitted the bracket and welded it into place, and the drivers resumed their record-making journey. Seventeen days after they had left Edmonton they reached Victoria. Their arrival in Kamloops sparked a wave of enthusiastic predictions about the city's future, but at remote, isolated Albreda, life continued to deteriorate at the Frye ranch.

Mike Frye was sitting on the woodpile beneath the eaves of the cabin when a railroad sectionman confronted his father on the yard. He called Fred Frye a liar over the count of a number of ties delivered to the railroad.

"No one calls me a liar," Fred returned, and launched himself at the man.

They were rolling in the dirt when suddenly blood showed on the sectionman's shoulder, and he screamed, clawing at Fred's face. Fred ripped his hands free, grabbed the man's head and shoulder and pushed him away, tearing the man's throat out with his teeth. A spray of blood mottled Fred's face. The man fell back, choking, blood flooding his throat. Fred kicked the man insensible, then carried the body off.

A train crew, seeking the missing man, found his abandoned speeder miles from the Frye homestead. Days later, they found the body, badly decomposed. The wounds about the throat were so terrible that they were ascribed to some animal, and the body was buried the same day. The decomposition of the corpse precluded any autopsy. Railroading was a dangerous business. During the 1920's, scarcely a week passed without the newspapers reporting at least one person killed in some manner on the railway. And bodies frequently washed up on the point in Kamloops, bloated and unrecognizable. Nevertheless, foul play was suspected and rumors began to circulate about how the man had met his death.

Edith dared not say anything about the fight reported by Mike; though she suspected the truth, a wife could not testify against her husband. The terror continued on the homestead.

Moonshine Madness

November swept in with cold winds and rain, and game was in rut. On November 14 Fred sent Charles and Frances out hunting; they were to go up Three Sisters mountain after caribou. Fred would go with them. They were glad to be able to get their drink-crazed father away from the homestead. Together, Charles and Frances could cope with him.

They made their way to a trapper's cabin and settled down for the night. Despite the fading daylight it was bright outside. The waxing moon rose over the mountains and flooded the woods with light. Frances and Charles made supper over the rusted tin woodstove in the cabin and made up their sleeping robes. Fred did not eat, but drank from a jar of moonshine. After a while he dropped the jar into his coat pocket and stood up.

"I'm going out to see if any game is moving," he told them.

Taking his shotgun, he went out into the night. He worked his way along the high bench above the valley, passing from meadow to meadow. The moon filtering through the threadbare foliage showed the way. Fred fought his way through the brush to the CN tracks far below, then turned back toward Albreda. From time to time he sipped from the jar.

The cabin was lit when he arrived; lantern light flowed through the windows and glittered on the frosted ground. He could hear Edith putting the children to bed. Fred crouched beneath a window and fumbled for a match. He held it up to the pane and struck it with his thumbnail, then jerked his hand down.

"There's a light at the window!" one of the children cried.

Edith's hackles rose as another match flared. "It's just your father, playing tricks," she said, trying to keep her voice calm.

Outside, Fred scratched at the door and growled, then howled like a wolf. He grew tired of the game when no one responded and came in. Edith put a plate on the table and heaped it with potatoes and meat. Fred ate, then took out the whisky and started drinking. He did not appear drunk, but Edith sensed the danger. She signalled to Ella to get the little children ready to sleep in the root cellar.

In the front room, Ella hurried to get the little ones dressed. Fred set down his bottle and yanked back the canvas curtain over the doorway. Ella jumped for the door, not quick enough, and Fred seized her. Edith tried to pry his hand from her arm but Fred flung her away and dragged Ella outside. He grabbed the girl by the neck and beat her head against the logs.

Edith ran out and tried to pry his hands away. Ella slid down, dazed, and crawled away as Fred seized Edith by the throat and bent her back beneath the small stand of jackpines that grew beside the door. Edith's eyes were bulging when Mike came out of the darkness with a piece of stovewood. He lifted the club and struck his father across the back of the neck. The burly man fell forward, then rolled down the bank.

"I've killed him!" Mike thought, horrified and elated. He dropped the club and ran.

When she found her breath Edith stood up, weakly. Ella was sitting against the wall, her head bruised and hair clotted with blood.

"Mother, I don't know why you didn't just drown us all," Ella told her.

"I love all of you," Edith said simply. "Now quick, take the babies out to the root house. Lock them in. Here's the key."

Ella wanted only to run, hide, and never return, but she could not abandon her mother and brothers and sisters. She did as Edith had bade. When she returned to the cabin she could hear Edith trying to rouse the unconscious man. When Fred crawled up the bank, wounded and ready to annihilate whoever had attacked him, she heard Edith trying to soothe him. Ella remained outside in the cold until late and Fred was incoherent with whisky. Edith finally wrestled him to bed, then lay down herself, bruised and exhausted.

Fred woke late the next morning, red-eyed and aching. The children had long since been fed and shooed outside; they did not need to be told to keep out of their father's way. Mike stayed well-hidden until he saw his father go out of the house.

Mike slipped into the cabin and went to his parents' bed in the kitchen. He slid the double-barreled shotgun from beneath the bed and loaded it, then laid it back exactly as it had been.

Fred returned with a quart-sized sealer of moonshine. Uncannily aware of a threat, he checked the shotgun. He removed the cartridges, laid the gun back, then settled at the kitchen table with his drink. He remained there all afternoon, and did not interfere when Edith made supper for the children. Edith hurried them outside after they had eaten. Ella stayed nearby, as she had been told. Mike came into the cabin again through the front door, and stayed in the front room until he heard his father's voice rise. There was the sound of a blow and a cry.

Mike ran in, seized the shotgun and leveled it at his father. As he thumbed back on hammer he knew something was wrong; Fred's reactions were far too relaxed. Fred wheeled on Mike, snatched the shotgun away, then took a piece of stovewood and thrashed the boy from his neck to his heels. No one dared move until he threw the stick aside and strode out.

Edith and Ella treated Mike's wounds, then locked him up with the other children. When Fred came in again he took some stew but stayed up drinking until late in the night. At last he went to bed and Edith lay down beside him. She could not sleep, seized by fear that something had happened to Charles and Frances.

Their father's disappearance had not unduly surprised Charles or Frances. He might have gotten lost, or more likely, he had gotten drunk and was sleeping it off somewhere nearby. He may have been sitting up, looking for game.

They hunted all the next day, becoming more and more concerned. At dusk they returned to the trapper's cabin, expecting to find their father there. A sick feeling descended over them when they found the cabin empty.

"He's gone home," Frances said.

Charles nodded. "We better get back early."

At dawn they shouldered their packs and headed for Albreda. It was mid-morning when they arrived, to find their parents still in bed. They cleaned their weapons and hung them up in the woodshed adjoining the kitchen, well above the reach of the little children.

Edith rose, relieved at their return, and made breakfast. She had Ella unlock the root cellar and bring the little ones out to eat. Fred rose but took no breakfast. He opened his sealer of moonshine and resumed drinking.

"Get anything?" he asked Charles and Frances.

They shook their heads.

"I want you to get back up there," he said. "Don't come back 'til you've got something, then we'll take a team up to pack it down."

Reluctantly, Charles and Frances went out again, and conferred in the yard.

"I don't want to go," whispered Frances. "He's in one of his moods again. We shouldn't leave Mother."

"We'll stay," Charles agreed.

They came in again, hung up their rifles and unloaded their packs.

Fred, befuddled and insane, sat at the kitchen table gulping from the sealer. The lunatic alchemy of the moonshine boiled in his veins. He could feel people peering at him through the windows, plotting, planning things against him. Edith was at the center of it all. He felt a flush of pity; they would all be better off dead. He would start with Edith, then all the others. Afterwards he would go home, back to Seattle, where people would be glad to see him. The short man groped to his feet, mumbling to himself, lapsing back into the Biblical phraseology he had absorbed when he was small.

Fumbling in his pocket he found his clasp knife and yanked the long blade open. Edith started at the movement and jumped for the door. Fred wrapped one great, sinewed arm around her throat. Edith squirmed, kicking, scratching at his forearm through the thick shirt and heavy woollen underwear. Frances and Charles ran in, threw themselves at Fred and worked the knife free. Frances threw the knife into the firebox of the woodstove. Together, they half carried, half dragged their crazed father to the bed. There they held him throughout the rest of the short winter afternoon, pleading with him to calm down until their words turned into a litany. It was like trying to hold a python, squirming and coiling, the great muscles working. At last, Fred seemed to relax. He slumped forward, breathing loudly. Frances and Charles relaxed their hold, but remained beside him.

Edith brought the little ones in to eat and Fred rose up, brushing Charles and Frances aside. He hit Edith with his closed fist, knocking her halfway across the kitchen into the woodbox; sticks of kindling flew. The little children scattered. Frances and Charles picked themselves up as Fred seized his shotgun and pointed it at Edith.

"This is the last time I shall load this," he intoned. "By morning we will all be with the little one."

He pointed through the wall at the family cemetery, as if his eyes could see through the logs to some unspeakable Hell beyond. As he stood in a trance Charles and Frances jumped for the shotgun and wrestled it away. Edith slid it back beneath the bed.

"I will send us all to meet him," Fred droned, undeterred. "I will slay us all."

He began to leap in place, great bounding jumps which brought his head close to the beams of the ceiling.

"I am God!" he bellowed in an enormous voice that shook the cabin. "God! There is no power greater than me! I am God!"

"Take the children out!" Edith commanded, pushing them before her into the woodshed.

Charles, Ella and Frances herded their little brothers and sister outside as Edith took Charles' rifle from its pegs. She threw the loading lever down, forced two cartridges into the rotary magazine and closed the lever, loading the breech. She could barely hear Fred's ranting over the pounding in her ears. She felt her body to be distant, but at the same time working with smooth co-ordination. She stepped into the open doorway, holding the rifle.

Fifteen feet away, Fred stooped by the bed, reaching for the shotgun. The intensity of sensation increased within Edith, her ears ringing. She lifted the long rifle toward the tormented husk of her husband. When the sights aligned on his head, she squeezed the trigger.

The butt of the rifle jolted her shoulder. Fred fell forward onto his face. He rolled onto his back, arms outspread. A thin trickle of blood ran down from his ear and pooled beneath his arm, then flowed to the trap door above the cellar. Edith lowered the rifle and stepped out to the woodshed where she hung it on its pegs. She went outside and found the children gathered.

"What have you done, Mother?" Frances quavered.

"I've shot your father," Edith replied. "I've shot your father."

The Investigation

The little children were clustered around Ella like chicks beside a hen. Edith knelt and took them in her arms.

"You don't have to be afraid of your dad any more," she said.

When she had calmed them she straightened. "Charlie, take the little ones to Stewarts' and tell him what has happened. Ask him to send for the police, and to come here. I'll wait here."

Charles picked up Fred Jr. and, followed by the others, walked into the darkness. The moon, less than a week from being full, gave enough light to see. Frances followed for a few yards, then turned and went into the house with Edith. Ella was nowhere to be seen.

A mile and a half down the road, Charles and the little children came into the light shining from Stewarts' window. The front room of the house was a store; tins of baking soda lined the window sill. Stewart came out when he heard the door open.

"Hullo, Charlie. What is it?"

"Mother shot Father," Charles blurted. "She told us

to come here and see if you would look after the little ones, and to send for the police. She wants you to come back."

"Good Lord! Shot dead?"

Charles nodded. Quick footsteps came from inside the house. Peter Stewart's wife had overheard. She swept the children inside while Stewart donned his coat.

They hurried to the CN depot, where Stewart dispatched a wire to the provincial police in Lucerne. Mr. Arnold, the operator, accompanied Stewart and Charles back to the homestead. Halfway there they found Frances standing on the road, and brought her with them.

Edith was sitting on a chair in a corner of the front room. Stewart went straight to her.

"Are you all right, Edith?"

The little woman swallowed and nodded, not looking at him. "I had to, Pete. Now they'll take me and who will look after the children? I don't know what they'll do to me, but if you'll look after them I'll find some way to pay you."

"Don't you worry about that," Stewart said, "they'll be just fine with us, and don't worry about pay. Edith, we all knew something was going on here. Fred was not in his right mind. We should have done something long ago. I will stand by you in court if need be."

Stewart and Arnold went into the back room, letting the canvas curtain fall behind them. The corpse was staring at the ceiling, eyes glazed. They tried to close the lids but they kept popping open, and the arms would not stay folded. They bound up the gaping jaw with a neckerchief and covered the body with a blanket from the bed.

They rejoined Edith in the front room. Charles brought in wood and stoked the heater. Arnold made his apologies and left.

Frances looked around. "Where's Ella?"

The younger girl's belongings were gone. Her boots were missing. Ella had fled.

The beacon of the morning train beat through the ice fog surrounding the Albreda depot the next day, and the whistle wailed. Two men emerged from the warmth of the train into the frigid haze. One wore the uniform of the British Columbia Provincial Police; the other carried a familiar black bag. They introduced themselves to the station agent as Constable Sinclair and Dr. Thomas F. O'Hagan.

They went directly to the Frye cabin, picking up a small body of men along the way, the curious and the morbid. The Albreda Glacier glowed in the morning light, a stupendous crystal filling the end of the valley. Sinclair went directly to the front door.

"I am Constable Sinclair, B.C. Provincial Police," he announced. "Mrs. Frye?"

Pete Stewart beckoned him in. Dr. O'Hagan followed.

"Where is the body?" Sinclair asked.

"In here." Stewart moved to block Edith's view and pushed back the canvas. The men went in. The kitchen stove had gone out and it was cold in the room. O'Hagan pulled back the blanket and they knelt by the body. The back of the head was clotted with blood. O'Hagan sheared the bandage holding the jaw shut and together they examined the wound. Sinclair returned to the front room.

"Mrs. Frye," he said formally, "you are under arrest. Anything that you say may be used against you."

Edith nodded. A great weight and darkness seemed to descend over her, constricting her chest and heart. She could hardly breathe.

"We have had a lot of trouble," she said in one long exhalation. After an aching interval, her lungs filled and the choking weight lifted. "He...he was going to kill us all. He tried to use a knife on me but they got it away from him. Finally I shot him."

"What did you use?" Sinclair asked.

"That gun," she said, pointing through the kitchen to the woodshed.

Sinclair went through the kitchen and found the rifle, Charles' pride and joy, a .303 Savage lever-action, one of the most modern firearms available. He threw open the action. A spent casing ejected and fell to the floor. Sinclair removed the remaining live cartridge and pocketed them both. Peering down the barrel, he noted the powder residue on the rifling. He confiscated the Savage and Edith's old .45-90 Winchester.

Sinclair made a thorough search of the cabin and found the shotgun beneath the bed, near the body. In a large wooden chest filled with clothing, he found a naturalization paper.

"Where's the moonshine?" Sinclair asked Charles.

"In the cupboard."

Sinclair found the sealer and unscrewed the lid. He sniffed, wrinkling his nose. "That's the real stuff, all right. Where did he get it?"

"He made it."

Dr. O'Hagan went out and returned with a group of men. Stooping, they picked up the body and followed the doctor out. The outstretched arms would not bend and they had to turn the corpse on its side to manoeuver it through the woodshed. They took the body to the barn and laid it on an improvised table of planks laid on sawhorses. While Dr. O'Hagan performed an autopsy, Sinclair made sketches of the cabin floorplan, including the location of the body. He lifted the trap door over the cellar and noted the wide bloodstain soaked into the earthen floor. When Sinclair was done inside the house he had Charles take him to the still, hidden in the willows by the spring.

"How long had he been making it?"

"All spring and summer," Charles said.

Shortly after noon, Sinclair swore six men and the doctor convened a coroner's inquest in the barn. Edith, Charles and Frances testified. Only one point remained to be cleared up.

"What happened to the knife?" Sinclair asked.

"We threw it in the stove," Charles said.

"Mr. Stewart, would you go get it?"

Stewart found the blackened knife in the cinders on the cold grate of the kitchen stove. Sinclair took the knife for evidence.

The verdict was inescapable. Frederick Charles Frye had died as a result of a bullet wound inflicted by his wife.

At the house, Sinclair formally charged Edith with murder, and informed her she would be taken into detention at McBride. The officer made sure the Frye children would be looked after until formal arrangements could be made.

At Albreda, the train whistle shrilled. Edith hugged her children and boarded the train north, perhaps never to return.

The news spread like wildfire. Some people, including Ella, never believed that Edith had fired the fatal shot. They blamed, or applauded, Charles.

An account of the finding of the coroner's jury was telegraphed to the *Kamloops Standard Sentinel.* The November 17 issue of the paper blared:

MRS. FRED FRYE KILLS HUSBAND

———•———

Well Known Member of Local Elks Shot Dead at His Albreda Ranch

———•———

WIFE CONFESSES TO SHOOTING AND IS TAKEN BY POLICE TO LUCERNE

———•———

A well known charter member of Kamloops Elks Lodge met a tragic death at his Albreda ranch 180 miles north of here on the CNR last night when he was shot dead by his wife. No details are procurable, although word was received here at 3.15 this afternoon that Mrs. Frye had been found guilty of murder by a coroner's jury at Albreda and had confessed to the shooting. She is on her way to Lucerne in charge of the provincial police.

Fred Frye, who was also a tie contractor. at Swift Creek, was very well known here and came regularly to town with Mrs. Frye and his seven children.

Those who knew him state that he was very good to his family while on those trips. He was 45 years of age and well-liked, a hard worker and expected his wife and children to take their share in duties of the camp and ranch.

Local Elks were much exercised over the news today and are awaiting particulars they have called for.

Three days later, on Monday, November 20, Inspector Parsons of the provincial police in Fort George arrived in Albreda. He spent the day making a thorough search of the homestead, sketching the buildings, inspecting the root cellar, fetid with the children's waste, and the still.

Dr. O'Hagan accompanied Inspector Parsons. He

conducted a post mortem.

The formal inquest was convened in the barn. Dr. O'Hagan gave his testimony, while Parsons took notes for the preliminary hearing to be held in McBride the following day.

After the inquest Pete Stewart took charge of the burial. They lowered Fred Frye into the ground near his infant son. The moon was full that night.

The killing of Fred Frye hit the front pages of the newspapers. The *Prince George Citizen* dispatched a reporter to McBride to cover the preliminary hearing. The story, in the Friday, November 24, issue read

THIS WOMAN FOUGHT FOR THE LIVES OF HER CHILDREN

———•———

Preliminary Hearing in Frye Murder Case Discloses a Condition in Which a Man Crazed With Liquor Kept His Family in Terror of Their Lives in Isolated Shack

———•———

The preliminary hearing of Mrs. Charles Frye, at McBride, on Tuesday, for the murder of her husband, uncovered a condition of affairs at the Frye homestead at Albreda which astounded all present. There was no doubt about the killing of Frye, or that he met death at the hands of his wife, but the marvel was that the killing did not take place sooner. The Frye family consisted of the husband, wife and seven children. The father seemingly divided his time between making ties and moonshine whisky, and the members of the family lived lives of terror for months. Half of the time Frye was out of his mind by reason of excessive drinking and from time to time made threats against the life of his wife.

Children Used Axes

———•———

All of the children who could handle an axe were obliged to work in the bush cutting ties for their father's account, and it is said to be a matter of record that the two elder girls, aged 15 and 17 years, became so proficient in tie-making that they established a record of thirty ties in one day.

The family lived in a two-roomed house, but frequently in his terrorizing, Frye would drive all of the chidlren out of the house and force them to sleep in a root-house without ventilation (sic) of any kind.

The household equipment included among other things, two rifles and a shotgun. On Tuesday Frye loaded his shotgun, and placed it under his bed, with threats to use it on his family. He was utterly crazed with liquor and the wife figured that it was his life or those of the rest of the family. Frye got off his bed and began groping for the shotgun under the bed. The wife reached for the rifle and sent the children out of the house. In a few minutes a shot rang out and Frye was killed.

Distressing Conditions

———•———

She was given a preliminary hearing on Tuesday before Thomas R. Lloyd, Justice of the Peace, and committed to Okalla (sic) prison pending trial on a charge of murder.

Inspector Parsons and Chief Constable McNeil conducted the prosecution and they agreed that they had never before encountered such distressing conditions. From the stories told by the Frye children, their lives and that of their mother must have been perfect hell for months, being constantly in fear of a drink-crazed father.

The police have made provision for a number of the children for the present, and if places for the others cannot be secured they will be placed in some provincial institution. In the meantime the mother will remain in jail until next spring unless some move is made to secure her liberty pending trial. The matter is referred to the women's organizations of Prince George for their investigation.

If the conditions the woman lived under for months past are half as bad as pictured, Mrs. Frye should not remain in jail for a single day.

The editor of the Kamloops Standard Sentinel, perhaps for reasons of space, but more likely in consideration of the feelings of the Kamloops Elks, omitted the final sentence when he reprinted the story from the *Citizen* in the November 28 issue. Nothing more was heard from the Kamloops Elks, but there was no financial aid forthcoming from the lodge; the particulars of the case which they had called for proved to be more than they had bargained for.

Edith was taken south to New Westminster and Oakalla Prison in care of a matron of police. Lottie was boarded with a family in Lucerne while the other little children stayed with the Stewarts. Frances and Charles returned to the homestead. The police issued a bulletin for Ella.

The story hit the front page of the *Prince George Citizen* again the next week, in the December 5 issue.

PRINCE GEORGE WOMEN TAKE UP THE CASE OF MRS. FRYE

———•———

Will Seek to Induce Attorney-General Manson to Release, Pending Trial, The

Woman who Killed a Drink-Crazed Husband to Save the Lives of Her Helpless Children

———•———

The women of Prince George have dedicated themselves to the welfare of Mrs. Charles F. Frye, who is in Okalla (sic) prison awaiting trial upon the charge of murdering her husband at the family homestead in the vicinity of Albreda.

The particulars of this case were particularly distressing. The Frye family consisted of eight children, seven of whom were living with their parents in conditions of unbelievable hardship for a country like British Columbia. All of the children, old enough to swing an ax, were forced by the father to work in the bush cutting ties, including two girls fifteen and seventeen years old. For months the father had been more or less out of his mind due to the consumption of home-brewed liquor and maintained a reign of terror by threatening from time to time to kill the entire family.

On the day of the murder, in the presence of the children, he had loaded a shot-gun and had told them he intended to use it on them. He placed the gun under his bed and lay down to sleep. There was no help at hand, and the mother, to ensure the safety of her children, secured possession of a rifle which was in the house, and then awaited developments.

When her husband got up from the bed, and with threats of his intended action commenced to grope under the bed for the shot-gun, Mrs. Frye sent a bullet from the rifle through his heart.

At the inquest which followed, and at the preliminary hearing at McBride, the story of the killing was told by the mother and children, and, according to legal formula, there was nothing but to commit Mrs. Frye to the Okalla (sic) prison to await her trial next summer. The family was pitiably poor, and without friends to interest themselves in the welfare of the mother who the law locked up for defending the lives of her children from their drink-crazed father.

The women of Prince George took action on Saturday when they commenced the circulation of a petition to Hon. A.M. Manson, attorney-general for the province, asking him to arrange for the release of Mrs. Frye pending the trial of case at the next court of assize in this city. The petition is in the hands of Mrs. J.H. Johnson and Mrs. G.G. McKenzie. It was circulated on Saturday at the bazaar of St. Michel's church, and in a short time the signatures of 125 women in attendance were secured. It is the intention to circulate the petition at all meetings of women held in this city in the next few days, and to deposit copies at the Prince George Drug Store and at Peck & Gillis' store on Third Avenue, where it may be signed by any woman desirous of doing so. The case will also be drawn to the attention of the women's organizations at the coast, and there is every reason to believe, when the circumstances are fully understood by the attorney-general, he will arrange to give Mrs. Frye her liberty.

By mid-December the signatures of 222 Prince George women had been taken, and the petition was mailed to Victoria. The Thursday, December 26, *Citizen* stated in its headlines:

PETITION IN THE CASE
OF MRS. FRYE IS
FAVORABLY RECEIVED

───────●───────

**Original Depositions Taken At
Preliminary Hearing Not Yet in
Victoria, But When They Come
to Hand Matter of Considering
Bail For Woman Will be Taken Up**

The last sentence of the story, giving the bare details of the case, noted, "...in the event of her being unable to secure counsel at the trial of her case, it will be the duty of the crown to appoint counsel to act for her."

Fred's family in California at first blamed Edith entirely for Fred's death, but when the facts began to emerge they relented. Frances was invited to stay with them in California until the trial, and she took the train to Hillside, near San Francisco.

Julius Bronson moved to Albreda to look after things. Still hale and hearty, he would build a cabin on a ridge high above the homestead, where Mike, in particular, would often climb to visit.

Mike, carrying his father's .45 Colt beneath his coat in a shoulder holster, worked a trapline some ten miles long, while Charles returned to Swift Creek to cut ties. Ella, meanwhile, was far from the valley. She could hold her own in the woods with any man, and she found her way to Vancouver Island where she hired on in a logging camp. The girl was afflicted with facial hair, and could pass for a man.

In January after a review by the attorney-general, Edith was released from prison. She returned to Albreda and found employment cooking at a logging camp about six miles from the homestead. She would walk home on weekends, bringing food.

A page 3 story in the April 26 *Citizen* noted:

Mrs. Edith Julia Frye, the woman who killed her husband at Albreda in November last, in defence of herself and her childre, and who received her liberty pending trial, as the result of the women of Prince George and vicinity, will be placed on trial in Kamloops. Stuart Henderson, of Victoria, will conduct her defence.

126

Henderson was a leading criminal court lawyer, who only lost two of the dozens of defences he undertook in British Columbia during his entire career.

Ella was finally located on Vancouver Island, subpoenaed to testify at the trial and returned to Albreda. The Fryes were ostracized by some members of the community. Parents forbade their children to play with the little Fryes, and passers-by would point out the "murder house."

On May 24 the Citizen announced in an inside page story:

WOMEN OF KAMLOOPS WILL RAISE FUNDS FOR DEFENSE OF MRS. EDITH FRYE

The spring assize court opens at Kamloops on Tuesday with Mr. Justice Murphy presiding, when, for the first time in the history of Kamloops, a woman will face a charge of murder. She is Mrs. Edith Julia Frye, widow of Charles Fred Frye, the contractor of Swift Creek, who was shot to death on November 22 last. The trial would have taken place at Prince George, but a change of venue to Kamloops was considered advisable.

For the first time women jurors may sit, several having been empanelled, but with the option of refusing duty.

At a meeting of representative women of Kamloops last week, it was agreed to raise funds for the defense of Mrs. Frye and to engage the services of A.D. McIntyre, barrister.

McIntyre had a formidable reputation. A prominent member of the Kamloops legal profession since 1898, he was considered an able lawyer but was not popular with other members of his profession or the public. After his death in 1934 the *Kamloops Standard Sentinel* wrote, somewhat uncharitably, "...his methods belonged to another age, they were those of an opportunist, bent on a single purpose, the carrying out of his wish in court."

The family reunited in May for the trial. Late in the month, Edith, Charles, Frances and Ella, accompanied by Pete Stewart, took the CNR south to Kamloops. Edith would be on trial for her life. Murder was a hanging offence.

The Trial

The case of *Regina versus Frye* was heard before Mr. Justice Denis Murphy of the B.C. Supreme Court. Murphy, 52 at the time, was a very well-known judge, and much respected. He was clean shaven with greying hair neatly cut, and a wide mouth above a firm chin.

The prosecutor was J. Ross Archibald, a prominent Liberal who had practiced in Kamloops for nearly ten years. Sixteen potential jurors were called, and McIntyre rejected four. The jurors were R.C. Campbell, Horace W. Dingwell, Robert H. Lynch, Grant Berger, R. Chetwynd, Frank J. Dumont, Andrew S. Howe, A.J. McDonald, W.F. Blackwell, Thos. Hudson, Robert A. Small and Harry A. Ferguson. Ferguson, a leading citizen who ranched at nearby Savona, was elected foreman of the jury.

When the jury was sworn and Edith led into the prisoner's box, Archibald opened the trial:

"Your honor, I intend to show from the evidence to be presented that the Frye family came in from the American side during the construction days.

"They took up a piece of land at Albreda on the

CNR. The place is not thickly settled, but communication with the outside world is fairly easy by means of the operators on the CNR.

"The morals and standards of living of the family were rather low, but they must be judged by the law. There are seven children in the family, of whom the boy of nineteen and the girls of seventeen and fifteen will be called to give evidence.

"Call Inspector Parsons, please."

A clerk pinned up a large map of the homestead and Parsons indicated the various buildings. He paused at the roothouse.

"What was the roothouse like?" Archibald queried.

"Damp and cold with no ventilation," Parsons answered. "On the left side of the door was a bed; on the other was the potato bin."

"Describe the cabin where the family lived."

"It was divided into two rooms, with a woodshed off the kitchen. The floors were rough-hewn logs. There were two beds; the mattresses were crude, just straw covered with sacks; a table, six chairs and the usual utensils."

"Did you make any other observations?"

"The whole place was very crude and unhealthy," the inspector testified, "the root cellar in particular."

Edith heard his words faintly but clearly, as though listening across a lake. She felt humiliated; the cabin was as clean as anyone could manage. But the roothouse, though, that was bad, she thought, remembering the fetid smell and the odor of old vegetables. The children had not been able to come out; they had had to use the corner of the roothouse for a toilet. She could not help that. A sense of oppression too vast to resist settled over Edith like a great weight.

Dr. O'Hagan was called to the stand. He gave the clerk a drawing of a man's torso, a path marked from the ear to the heart. The clerk pinned the drawing up next to the map.

"Describe what you found at the inquest at the barn," Archibald said.

Dr. O'Hagan consulted a small notebook. "I found a circular wound behind the ear. It went down the left side of the neck, tearing the jugular vein, breaking through the left lung and entering the heart; the bullet was just under the skin. I took out the bullet."

"What was the cause of death?"

"Hemorrhage caused by bullet wound. The organs appeared to be in a healthy condition."

Constable Sinclair took the stand after O'Hagan stepped down. He swore to tell the truth and kissed the Bible. The jury foreman, Harry Ferguson, wrote something on a slip of paper.

"Give the position of the body," Archibald continued.

"It was lying just inside the door, on the back, with hands about two feet from the body. A small stream of blood was beside it."

"What did you do then?"

"I returned to the front room and spoke to Mrs. Frye. She didn't seem to take much interest. I told her she was under arrest and anything she might say may be used against her.

"She told me they had had a lot of trouble. The day before, Mr. Frye had threatened to kill them all. He had tried to use a knife on her but they got it away from him and put it in the stove, and finally she shot him. I asked her what she had shot him with and she said 'That gun' and pointed to a rifle on the wall."

"What style of rifle was it?"

"A .303 Savage. It was hanging on the east end of the building in which they lived, north of the entrance, about five and a half feet from the floor. I opened the rifle and found an empty cartridge case in the chamber, and one loaded cartridge."

"What did you do with the rifle?"

"I took possession and removed a double-barreled shotgun from under the bed and found another rifle."

"When did you find the shotgun?"

"About ten minutes after finding the first rifle. It was about ten inches under the bed."

"Was the body fully clothed?"

"It was."

The prosecutor held up a quart-sized fruit jar half

filled with a yellowish liquid. "Can you identify this object?"

"That is a sealer I took from the cupboard, but the liquid was colorless when I found it. It was moonshine."

"How did you know it was moonshine?"

"From the taste and smell. The boy showed me a still which his father had operated."

"Thank you. No further questions."

McIntyre rose. "Did you know Frye?" he asked the policeman.

"I have met him," Sinclair answered.

"He was a tie contractor?"

"So I have heard," the policeman replied exactly.

"Mrs. Frye appeared dejected?"

"She did."

"During the conversation you warned her that she was under arrest. Are you certain that she knew who you were, and fully understood your warning?"

"Yes."

"Was Mrs. Frye in a very nervous condition?"

"Yes."

"Had you any doubt she was telling the truth?"

"None at all."

McIntyre consulted his notes, a long pad of foolscap. "You examined the body for wounds and found only a scratch on the nose? You said at the preliminary that it was skinned for about an inch."

"Yes."

"You swore that Mrs. Frye told you there had been trouble for about three months; that Frye had threatened to kill her and the children several times, and that the trouble was caused by his drinking moonshine?"

"Yes."

"Was the roothouse as bad as described by Inspector Parsons?"

"It was a lot worse."

"Thank you. I have no more questions of this witness. Call Mr. Stewart, please."

Peter Stewart took the stand and swore to tell the truth.

"Please tell us what happened on the night of

November sixteenth," said McIntyre.

"I was at home the evening of November sixteen when Charlie Frye came and told me his mother had shot his dad, and would I come. I went to the depot and wired for a doctor and the police and then went to the Frye homestead. Mr. Arnold, the operator, came with me.

"We picked up Frances Frye on the road. Edith Frye was sitting in the front room. I saw the body, lying on its back.

"We, Mr. Arnold and I, tried to close the eyes but they wouldn't stay. We tied up the jaw and folded the arms. Mrs. Frye asked me to stay and I stayed all night."

McIntyre nodded to Archibald, who continued the questioning.

"How long did you know the victim?"

"I knew Fred Frye for ten or eleven years."

"Can you identify this object?" Archibald held up a fire-blackened clasp knife.

"That is the knife I took from the stove."

"Mr. Frye was a tie and pole contractor?"

"Yes."

"What kind of man was he?"

"About four foot eight or ten, powerfully built and very strong; a man to be feared in a scrap. He was frequently intoxicated and when drunk went nearly crazy, fairly ran amok."

"How did you find the knife?"

"Mrs. Frye told about it at the coroner's inquest and the doctor told me to take it out of the stove."

Stewart stepped down and Harry Ferguson, the jury foreman, handed a slip of paper to the court clerk. Mr. Justice Murphy read the note, then handed it back to the clerk.

"Some members of the jury would like to question the doctor again," he said. "Dr. O'Hagan, will you please take the stand? You are still sworn."

When he had taken the witness stand, the judge asked, "Dr. O'Hagan, how was the victim standing when shot? Could you determine that from the course of the wound?"

O'Hagan nodded. "I would say that the victim was

stooping when shot. The path of the bullet shows that he was below the level of the person who shot him."

"Could he have been stooping to take the shotgun from beneath the bed?"

"It was quite possible for him to have been reaching for the shotgun."

Charlie Frye took the stand next. There was a murmur of surprise when he told the court he was nearly twenty years old. The *Kamloops Standard Sentinel* reporter described him as "a stripling no larger than most boys of fifteen."

"Tell us what happened on the sixteenth of November last year," Archibald said.

The boy took a deep breath. "My sister, Frances, and I went back to the place after hunting. We were out two days. We went out with my father but he left us out there.

"When we got home, Mother and Father were still in bed, in the kitchen. Mother got up in about half an hour and made something for us to eat. Then Father got up and commenced drinking; he didn't eat anything.

"He told us to go out hunting again and we took our guns and went outside, but Frances didn't think it was safe to leave so we came back. We cleaned the guns and hung them up.

"Then Father started cursing and tried to cut Mother, but Frances and I, we got the knife away and threw it in the stove. We held him most of the afternoon.

"About suppertime he got away and knocked Mother into the woodbox and hit Ella with a stick of wood. He didn't eat anything.

"He took the shotgun out from under the bed and loaded it. He said it was the last time he would load it and he showed us the baby's grave and said we would all be with it by morning. He pointed the shotgun at Mother but we got it away and put it back under the bed.

"Mother told me to take all the children out so they wouldn't get hurt. We heard a shot and went back. Father was lying on the floor and Mother had my gun."

"Was the rifle loaded or unloaded when you went out?"

133

Charles swallowed. "Unloaded."

"How far was your mother from your father."

"About fifteen feet."

"What happened then?"

"Mother told us to go to Mr. Stewart's and report that Father was shot. He came back with us."

"What was your father doing when you went out of the house?"

"Jumping up and falling back."

"How long had he been drinking?"

"About three months. He said he would hurt some of the children sometime."

"Did your father exhibit a bad temper?"

"He had a bad temper when he was sober but he went crazy when he had liquor."

"How long had this particular drunk lasted?"

"About three days. Father said that he was going to kill us all. He said he was God and there was no power greater than him."

"Is it true that you never heard your mother say anything about killing your father?"

"Yes," said Charles.

Frances was called to the stand. Her testimony followed Charles' closely.

"What happened when you got back?" Archibald asked, toward the end of his examination.

"I asked Mother what she had done and she said, 'I've shot your father.' "

"Did you see your father load the shotgun?"

"Yes."

"Were you afraid of him?"

"We were all in terror of him."

"Thank you." Archibald went back to his table.

McIntyre rose. "Did your father force you to work?"

"He made Ella and me do a man's work making ties."

"What did you use?"

"An ax."

"How many did you make?"

Frances shrugged. "Couldn't say, exactly. More than a thousand, anyway."

Frances stepped down and Ella trudged into the courtroom. She stood stolidly in the witness box, a husky figure in her frock. The *Sentinel* reporter wrote "...her face had a worn, joyless look which sat ill on a girl just on the threshhold of life. Her testimony was on a line with that of her brother and sister."

"Why did you work at making ties?" McIntyre asked when Archibald had finished his questioning.

"Father made us," Ella said flatly.

"Her answer was expressive of much that was unsaid," the *Sentinel* reporter wrote.

"What was your father doing with the knife?"

"Trying to cut my mother's throat."

"Why was the shotgun taken away from your father?"

"He pointed it at Mother and threatened to shoot us all with it."

"Thank you," McIntyre concluded.

"That concludes the Crown's case against Mrs. Frye," Archibald said, half rising from his chair.

McIntyre addressed the judge. "I request that the indictment be quashed. The Crown has failed to produce evidence to prove its case."

"Mr. McIntyre, that is a matter for the jury to decide," Mr. Justice Murphy ruled.

"Very well," McIntyre said. "I call for my first witness Robert G. Patterson of this city."

Patterson, owner of the *Kamloops Telegraph*, took the stand. He stated he had been a resident of the city for eleven years.

"Where did you first meet the deceased?" McIntyre asked.

"I met Fred Frye in the Elks Club some years ago. He was under the influence of liquor and I had to take him to his boarding house."

"An objection!" Archibald called.

"Not sustained," the judge ruled. "The character of the victim is of considerable relevance in this instance."

McIntyre proceeded. "What did you do when you got the deceased to his room?"

"I had great difficulty getting him to his room. When

we were there he produced a quart jar half full of alcohol from which he drank. He poured some in a saucer and lit it to prove that it was pure."

"Did he behave like an ordinary drunk?"

"He was more like a crazy man."

"Thank you. Call P.J. Stewart."

"The witness is still sworn," the judge advised as Stewart resumed the stand.

"How long have you known the Fryes?"

"Ten or twelve years. There are quite a few people living in the country around Albreda."

"What is Mrs. Frye's reputation?"

"She is considered a good, honest, hard-working woman. Her reputation is of the best."

"Thank you. No further questions of this witness. Please call Mrs. Frye to the stand."

There was a stir in the courtroom as Edith stepped into the witness box. She looked tired and discouraged. Her dark eyes seemed very bright. She laid her hand on the thick Bible and swore to tell the truth.

"How long were you married?" McIntyre asked gently.

"We were married for nearly twenty-three years."

"And how long have you lived in Albreda?"

"We lived in Canada for about nineteen years," Edith said. "We came here from Alberta where we were raising stock."

"What was your husband's character?"

Edith took a long, trembling breath. "He was always a drinking man. He shot a man in a drunken quarrel before we came to Canada. Everyone was afraid of him when he had liquor."

"How long had he been making moonshine on this occasion?"

"Since last spring. He was hardly sober from one time to another. When Charles and Frances went hunting he went with them, but he came back and tried to frighten the children.

"He came in and got supper and then started to beat Ella. He took her outside and knocked her head against the wall. I tried to stop him and he choked me. He

136

quarreled all night and stayed up the next day and the next night.

"I had got him quieted down a little when Frances and Charles came home the next day. Frances didn't think it safe to leave. They held him all afternoon to keep him from doing damage.

"He always kept the shotgun under the bed. Sometimes he would get up at night to scare away marauders. When he broke away from Frances and Charles he showed us all the baby's grave and said he would send us all to join the little one. Finally he began jumping up and down in the middle of the room and screaming threats.

"I sent the children out with Charles and got his rifle down and loaded it. I went back to see what he was doing. When I got to the door he was reaching for the shotgun under the bed and I shot. I heard the gun drop and he fell to the floor. Then I sent for the police."

"You fired one shot. Was it in fear for your life?" McIntyre asked.

"Certainly. If he had got that gun we would all have been dead."

"How long had this drunk continued?"

"I had been up with him every night for nearly three months."

"Do you dispute what the constable says you told him?"

"No," said Edith very quietly.

"How long were you in confinement in prison?"

"About two months. Since then I have been living with my family."

"I have no further questions," McIntyre said, and sat down.

Archibald rose. "Did you load the rifle before he grabbed the shotgun?"

"Yes."

"When you were talking with the Lucerne constable you said nothing about Frye reaching for the shotgun."

"He said not to tell him anything as it would be used against me."

"If he had been continually abusing you, why didn't you appeal to the police? There was an operator at

Albreda."

"He wouldn't let me away from the house, and besides, a number of times complaints were made to the police about moonshining and it didn't do any good."

"So you didn't think British law sufficient to look after you. Wasn't it true that there were three grownups against one?"

"We were not against him. We were merely trying to keep him from doing damage," Edith answered, her voice shaking.

"Why did you send the children out?"

"I didn't want them to get hurt." Edith's voice broke and she blinked back tears. "If they could have been cared for I would rather I had been shot, but he would not have cared for them. I did it to save the children."

People in the public gallery were dabbing at their eyes.

"No more questions," Archibald said.

Edith stepped down from the witness stand. The reporters scribbled furiously. After the commotion had settled, McIntyre rose and made his appeal to the jury.

"You are charged with trying a fellow citizen for the highest crime. That responsibility should keep any jury on tenterhooks, especially when they must pass on the motives of the opposite sex.

"This is the case of a wife and husband, and the character of both should be well weighed. You should also take into account the effect of liquor on various people. Where it merely makes fools of some men, it makes maniacs of others, and especially the stuff called moonshine, which contains a poison known as fusel oil.

"You have heard the reputation given the wife by her neighbors, and that given to the husband-father, who forced his own children to sleep in the roothouse and otherwise used them as an animal would not use its young. You the jury should remember that she did this to defend her children, and the first thing she did afterwards was to send for the police.

"She has stated that her husband was reaching for the shotgun. The coroner's testimony confirms that he was shot while in a crouching position. Luckily for her,

138

that shot was fatal. If it had not been, she today would be under the sod and Fred Frye facing trial for murder.

"I give the prisoner unto your hands, confident that you will do her justice. In the words of the oldest lawbook, 'Quit you like men.' "

The prosecutor bore the handicap of opposing a tiny woman who clearly had won the sympathy of the jury and the public.

Archibald said, "It is not so much Mrs. Frye that is on trial here as it is the question of whether the British Empire, which would send its army to the ends of the earth to protect its humblest subject, is able to protect the women of British Columbia.

"Perhaps Frye was all that the accused claimed he was, but the question is, did he come to his death in the right manner? The family lived in deplorable circumstances, but they should still abide by the law. I look to you, the jury, to bring in a verdict which will show that British law is sufficient under all circumstances."

When Archibald had sat down Mr. Justice Murphy turned in his high seat to instruct the jury.

"There are three courses open to you. You may find the prisoner guilty of murder; guilty of manslaughter; or not guilty. The verdict is not a matter of choice. You have taken an oath to justly try the case on the evidence submitted, and on nothing else. You are not trying a system of law, but whether or not the prisoner at the bar is guilty."

He opened the Criminal Code and read out the definition of murder:

"Culpable homicide is murder if the offender means to cause the death of the person killed, or if the offender means to cause to the person killed any bodily injury which is known to the offender to be likely to cause death, and is reckless whether death ensues or not. That is the legal definition. Now, the law recognizes certain cases where one person is entitled to kill one another. Every person unlawfully assaulted is entitled to use force to repel force even if he causes death, and to use that force to prevent any person from commiting a crime for which he could be arrested without warning.

"You cannot find the prisoner guilty of manslaughter, for it is admitted that she knew the wound would cause death. Your verdict must be either murder or acquittal.

"British law presumes every man innocent until proven guilty. The crime must be proven beyond a reasonable doubt. It is better that ninety-nine persons escape than one innocent man be condemned, and the burden of proof is laid upon the Crown. Unless you are convinced of the guilt of the accused beyond a reasonable doubt, you must bring in a verdict of acquittal."

The jurymen's feet rattled on the platform as they sidled out. They filed out of the courtroom and entered a jury room across the hall. A sheriff stood guard in front of the door. The court was adjourned to await the jury's decision.

Barely fifteen minutes after retiring, the jury emerged. The clerk called the court to order. Ferguson handed a sheet of paper to the clerk, who gave it to the judge. The judge scanned the page, wrote briefly in his ledger, and gave it back to the clerk.

In a loud voice the clerk read, "We find the defendant not guilty."

A wave of applause and foot stamping shook the courtroom. Edith stood dazed in the prisoner's box as the sheriff called for order. Mr. Justice Murphy rapped his gavel sharply several times.

"The prisoner is discharged," said the judge.

Epilogue

Edith Julia Frye returned to Albreda to care for her children. She continued to cook at the logging camp, returning home on weekends.

Her trials had not ended. She fought a forest fire, cutting fire lines with team and plow. She killed a wolf with a hatchet in the icy, rushing waters of Camp Creek. She became known for her good works, helping new settlers in the area adapt and survive. Neighbors who were young at the time still remember her walking through the drifts in the coldest weather, with no better footwear than canvas shoes and burlap sacks wrapped around her legs.

When her children were grown she remained at the homestead with her eldest son, Charles, until his death by drowning in 1950. Thereafter, she stayed with Jule and his family at Valemount, near the Swift Creek logging site a few miles north of Albreda, and often visited for varying periods with her other children who lived in the vicinity.

She died in Kamloops Hospital on May 15, 1956, at the age of eighty-three, from a malignant abdominal tumor probably caused by lack of proper medical care during childbirth. She was buried in the family cemetery at Albreda, near the boulder which stands above the highway.

Sources

Whisky and Wild Women, by Cy Martin
Booze, by James H. Gray
The Canadian Northern Railway, by T.D. Regehr
History of the Canadian Pacific Railway, by
     W. Kaye Lamb
Ocean to Ocean, by the Rev. Sanford Fleming (1872)
Kamloops Standard Sentinel, 1922–23
Prince George Citizen, 1922–23
McCumber Herald, 1905–06

Index